MW00472980

BD

New Essays on Hawthorne's Major Tales examines in detail some of Hawthorne's most important and most beloved stories such as "Young Goodman Brown," "Roger Malvin's Burial," "The Minister's Black Veil," "My Kinsman, Major Molineux," "Rappaccini's Daughter," and "Ethan Brand." The essayists make fresh attempts to probe the complex meanings of these much discussed works, utilizing a variety of contemporary critical methods. Michael Colacurcio argues for Hawthorne's interest in history; David Leverenz traces Hawthorne's mythopoeic interest in damnation and relates it to the tensions of Hawthorne's own time; Carol Bensick defends and admits the limitations of the identification of allusion in Hawthorne; Edgar Dryden explores Hawthorne's sense of traditional genre and relates it to modern hermeneutics; and Rita Gollin connects patterns of language with the psychological and biographic. Millicent Bell's introduction analyzes Hawthorne's early aspirations, places his writing in the context of contemporary audience expectations, and surveys the history of critical response to the tales from the writer's own time to our own.

NEW ESSAYS ON HAWTHORNE'S MAJOR TALES

GENERAL EDITOR
Emory Elliott
University of California, Riverside

Other books in the series:
New Essays on The Scarlet Letter
New Essays on The Great Gatsby
New Essays on Adventures of Huckleberry Finn
New Essays on Moby-Dick
New Essays on Uncle Tom's Cabin
New Essays on The Red Badge of Courage
New Essays on The Sun Also Rises
New Essays on A Farewell to Arms
New Essays on The American
New Essays on The Portrait of a Lady
New Essays on Light in August
New Essays on The Awakening
New Essays on Invisible Man
New Essays on Native Son
New Essays on Their Eyes Were Watching God
New Essays on The Grapes of Wrath
New Essays on Winesburg, Ohio
New Essays on Sister Carrie
New Essays on The Rise of Silas Lapham
New Essays on The Catcher in the Rye
New Essays on White Noise
New Essays on The Crying of Lot 49
New Essays on Walden
New Essays on Poe's Major Tales

New Essays on
Hawthorne's Major Tales

Edited by
Millicent Bell

CAMBRIDGE
UNIVERSITY PRESS

Published by the Press Syndicate of the University of Cambridge
The Pitt Building, Trumpington Street, Cambridge CB2 1RP
40 West 20th Street, New York, NY 10011-4211, USA
10 Stamford Road, Oakleigh, Melbourne 3166, Australia

First published 1993

Printed in the United States of America

Library of Congress Cataloging-in-Publication Data

New essays on Hawthorne's major tales / edited by Millicent Bell.
p. cm. – (The American novel)
Includes bibliographical references (p.   ).
ISBN 0-521-41837-2 (hardback). – ISBN 0-521-42868-8 (pbk.)
1. Hawthorne, Nathaniel, 1804–1864 – Criticism and interpretation.
I. Bell, Millicent. II. Series.
PS1888.N39   1993
813'.3 – dc20   92-44764

A catalog record for this book is available from the British Library.

ISBN 0-521-41837-2 hardback
ISBN 0-521-42868-8 paperback

Contents

v

Contents

5

Historicizing Hell in Hawthorne's Tales

DAVID LEVERENZ

page 101

6

Through a Glass Darkly:
"The Minister's Black Veil" as Parable

EDGAR A. DRYDEN

page 133

Notes on Contributors
page 151

Selected Bibliography
page 153

Series Editor's Preface

In literary criticism the last twenty-five years have been particularly fruitful. Since the rise of the New Criticism in the 1950s, which focused attention of critics and readers upon the text itself – apart from history, biography, and society – there has emerged a wide variety of critical methods which have brought to literary works a rich diversiy of perspectives: social, historical, political, psychological, economic, ideological, and philosophical. While attention to the text itself, as taught by the New Critics, remains at the core of contemporary interpretation, the widely shared assumption that works of art generate many different kinds of interpretations has opened up possibilities for new readings and new meanings.

Before this critical revolution, many works of American literature had come to be taken for granted by earlier generations of readers as having an established set of recognized interpretations. There was a sense among many students that the canon was established and that the larger thematic and interpretative issues had been decided. The task of the new reader was to examine the ways in which elements such as structure, style, and imagery contributed to each novel's acknowledged purpose. But recent criticism has brought these old assumptions into question and has thereby generated a wide variety of original, and often quite surprising, interpretations of the classics, as well as of rediscovered works such as Kate Chopin's *The Awakening*, which has only recently entered the canon of works that scholars and critics study and that teachers assign their students.

The aim of The American Novel Series is to provide students of American literature and culture with introductory critical guides to American novels and other important texts now widely read and studied. Usually devoted to a single work, each volume begins with an introduction by the volume editor, a distinguished authority on the text. The introduction presents details of the work's composition, publication history, and contemporary reception, as well as a survey of the major critical trends and readings from first publication to the present. This overview is followed by four or five original essays, specifically commissioned from senior scholars of established reputation and from outstanding younger critics. Each essay presents a distinct point of view, and together they constitute a forum of interpretative methods and of the best contemporary ideas on each text.

It is our hope that these volumes will convey the vitality of current critical work in American literature, generate new insights and excitement for students of American literature, and inspire new respect for and new perspectives upon these major literary texts.

Emory Elliott
University of California, Riverside

1

Introduction

MILLICENT BELL

HAWTHORNE began his literary career as a writer of short stories and for a long time feared he would never do anything else. It is true that at Bowdoin College he had begun an apprentice novel, *Fanshawe,* which he published a couple of years later anonymously and at his own expense. But, seeing its obvious defects, he forbade the few who knew about it ever to mention his authorship, and even his wife did not learn of its existence until after his death. For the ten years following his graduation – 1825 to 1835 – he seems to have plugged away at writings which he hoped might make a book of connected tales. He lived at home with his mother, saving expense, so he could persevere in this effort despite discouraging responses from publishers, and for some years later, even when he took on more self-sustaining work, he clung to the idea. His desire to make his literary reputation as the author of such a volume was not realized though he attempted it at least three times; we know for certain only the suggestive titles of these projects. We can guess at their overall schemes but are not really sure of the anticipated contents though portions survived to be published separately.[1]

The earliest such conception was a series called "Seven Tales of My Native Land," the manuscript of which he later claimed he shoved into the fire in disgust at the rebuffs it had received, and we have merely his sister Elizabeth's recollection that it contained stories involving old local legends about witchcraft or the traditions of New England sailing and piracy. One story supposed to have escaped destruction was published as "Alice Doane's Appeal" at the end of the Salem period. By that time he was planning another volume to be called "Provincial Tales," which would seem definitely to have been an imaginative investigation into the past of his native region; it probably would have included "The Wives of the Dead," "Roger Malvin's Burial," "My Kinsman, Major Molineux," and "The Gentle Boy." These stories he contributed instead to the 1832 issue of *The Token*, one of those Victorian annuals called "gift books," which came out every year in time for the Christmas trade. *The Token* was edited by the alertly commercial Samuel Griswold Goodrich, whose advice to Hawthorne may be reproduced as advice given the fictional Oberon in "The Devil in Manuscript": "No American publisher will meddle with an American work, seldom if by a known writer, and never if by a new one."[2] At Goodrich's urging, Hawthorne surrendered any immediate hope of his book, letting the four stories appear anonymously in the gift book. Still, the idea of making his reputation with a hard-covered volume with his name on the title page – a book perhaps possessing some unified focus – did not die easily. Two years later he conceived the idea of "The Story Teller," short compositions loosely linked by the adventures of a wandering storyteller. This too failed to interest the marketers of American books.

Hawthorne appears instead to have allowed these projects to be cannibalized as he was forced to sell off their intended components one by one to periodicals, in which they were printed anonymously. Some sense of his literary existence might be promoted by labeling a piece as "by the author of" something else that had proved popular, like "The Gray Champion" or "The Gentle Boy." But not until 1836 did a reviewer of the current *Token* identify in print the common authorship of a number of pieces that had appeared in its pages. He called Hawthorne's style "more pleasing, more fascinating, than any one's except . . . dear Geoffrey Crayon [Washington Irving],"[3] linking Hawthorne, as many subsequent reviewers would, with the writer whose successful collections of sketches and tales had made him famous.

Hawthorne's first published story, "The Hollow of the Three Hills," was a witchcraft tale perhaps of the kind his sister remembered as part of "Seven Tales of My Native Land." It appeared in his hometown newspaper, *The Salem Gazette*, in 1830, when he was twenty-six. He continued until 1850 to write brief fictions, despite some periods when he stopped writing altogether: when he was working as an editor of the *American Magazine of Useful and Entertaining Knowledge* in 1836 or as a Weigher and Gauger at the Boston Custom House from 1839 to 1841, participating in the communal life of the utopian colony of Brook Farm in 1841, or serving as Surveyor in the Salem Custom House from 1846 to 1849. Between 1830 and 1852, about a hundred of his tales and sketches appeared in print; then his interest in writing short pieces dropped. The success of *The Scarlet Letter* in 1850 changed his life. Henceforth he would write novels, or, as he called them, romances, of book length.

In the "Custom House" preface to *The Scarlet Letter,* the first of the four longer fictions he completed before his death, he imagines one of his Puritan ancestors murmuring contemptuously, "What is he? A writer of story-books!"[4] The Puritan reproach of triviality or digression from a better way of glorifying God might have been leveled against the writer of any fiction, short or long, but "story" is here an ambiguous generic term. Hawthorne probably felt, for his own reasons, that he had hardly, till then, done anything impressive, simply written one little tale or sketch after another for twenty years. Though he had published *books* by this time, they were not the thematically unified collections he had dreamed of. *Twice-Told Tales,* which came out in 1837 only because his friend Horatio Bridge had underwritten it without telling him, was reissued in 1842 by another publisher, with added gleanings from his buried periodical contributions, and a new collection of his tales old and new, *Mosses from an Old Manse,* came out in 1846.

Only rarely did the stories bear traces of the writer's persistent aspiration for something larger and more likely to launch him as a recognized author, like the four stories called "Legends of the Province House," printed in separate issues of the *Democratic Review* in 1838 and 1839, and then formed into a small subset of the second edition of *Twice-Told Tales.* "Egotism, or The Bosom Serpent" and "The Christmas Banquet," first printed in the same magazine and reprinted in *Mosses from an Old Manse,* may have been intended for another series, if we take seriously the subtitle of both — "From the unpublished 'Allegories of the Heart.' " More wistfully still, the second edition of the *Mosses* volume contained "Passages from a Relinquished Work," first published in the *New*

England Magazine twenty years earlier, probably a part of the sacrificed "Story Teller" project. "Fragments from the Journal of a Solitary Man," also from "The Story Teller" and given to the *New England Magazine* in the same period, was never republished in Hawthorne's lifetime. His uneasiness with the isolated short story – his sense that it was at best a "fragment" of something larger and better – was still suggested in the subtitle of "Ethan Brand," written almost at the same time as *The Scarlet Letter* and intended to be published along with it – "A Chapter from an Abortive Romance."

Even when his stories began at last to appear in collections bearing his name, Hawthorne felt that he ought to be writing another kind of book. "The Old Manse," with which he introduced his *Mosses*, deplored the writer's failure to produce something substantial, a treatise of morality, a work of history, or, "in the humblest event . . . a novel, that should evolve some deep lesson, and should possess physical substance enough to stand alone" (1124). Slightness and lightness instead of weightiness are qualities literal as well as figurative in his regrets. At the end of a period of particular personal happiness, his honeymoon in the Old Manse, he had published twenty-one stories. But he reported: "The treasure of intellectual gold, which I hoped to find in our secluded dwelling, had never come to light." "No profound treatise of ethics – no philosophic history – no novel, even, that could stand, unsupported, on its edges. All that I had to show, as a man of letters, were these few tales and essays, which had blossomed out like flowers in the calm summer of my heart and mind. . . . These fitful sketches, with so little of external life about them, yet claiming no profundity of purpose, – so reserved, even while they sometimes seem so frank, – often but half in earnest, and never, even when most so, expressing satisfactorily the thoughts which they profess to image – such trifles, I truly feel, afford no solid basis for a literary reputation. Nevertheless, the public – if my limited number of readers, whom I venture to regard rather as a circle of friends, may be termed a public – will receive them the more kindly, as the last offering, the last collection of this nature, which it is my purpose ever to put forth. Unless I could do better, I have done enough in this kind" (1148–9).

He did not, in fact, keep to this promise, but as he scooped up once more some of his fugitive short pieces for his last collection, *The Snow Image and Other Twice-Told Tales*, he had very little to add that had not been written by 1845; only "Ethan Brand," "The Great Stone Face," and the title story had been written and published in magazines while he was rapidly turning out *The House of the Seven Gables* and *The Blithedale Romance*. For the third time he deprecated his tales and other short works with the promise to his readers "these are the last" (1157) — and they virtually were, though he wrote one more story, "Feathertop," just in time to get it into *The Snow Image* in 1852.

It was not quite true that his early stories had left him "the obscurest man of letters in America" (1150), as he said in the preface to the third edition of *Twice-Told Tales*, published in 1851. But Poe was right when he wrote, after *Mosses*, that Hawthorne was still *"the* example, *par excellence,* in this country, of the privately-admired and publicly unappreciated man of genius."[5] Once identified as the author of his published collections, he was always reviewed warmly, and prized by the few and knowing, but these books sold modestly, so that he hardly "could regard himself as addressing the American Public, or, indeed, any Public at all" (1151). The treasure he failed to find at the Old Manse was not merely of "intellectual gold" but of money.[6] There had even been a not-so-blissful moment in 1844 when he had had to send his wife and new baby to live with her parents while he went back to his mother's house. It was a reproduction of that humiliating dependency his mother herself had suffered when, with her orphans, she had been forced to move in with her own family during his childhood.

Before these collections of stories appeared, he had not been visible even to the few. As he published *The Snow Image*, he looked back at his earliest years with the feeling that Bridge's intervention had saved him from complete obscurity. "Was there ever such a weary delay in obtaining the slightest recognition from the public, as in my case? I sat down by the wayside of life, like a man under enchantment, and a shrubbery sprung up around me, and the bushes grew to be saplings, and the saplings became trees, until no exit appeared possible, through the entangling depths of my obscurity. And there, perhaps, I should be sitting at this moment,

5

with the moss on the imprisoning tree-trunks, and the yellow leaves of more than a score of autumns piled above me, if it had not been for you" (1155).

This description has a very conventional sound, and it is a part of Hawthorne's self-dramatization. His complaint that he has lost connection with common life like a man lost in the woods and under some strange enchantment makes him a familiar nineteenth-century literary type, the Romantic Solitary. It is the tale he likes best, told in many of his stories from "The Minister's Black Veil" and "Wakefield" to "Ethan Brand." But one can take his remarks as a metaphoric description of an American writer's real experience in the changing literary market of the 1830s and 1840s. "What do you think of my becoming an Author, and relying for support upon my pen. . . . How proud you would feel to see my works praised by reviewers, as equal to the proudest productions of the scribbling sons of John Bull," he wrote his mother when he was preparing for Bowdoin in 1821. "But authors are always poor devils, and therefore Satan may take them," he answered for himself.[7] He had reason to fear that the American market offered little guarantee of success to a native writer when publishers could pirate and sell the popular British novelists of the day without having to pay for the privilege.

True, American novelists were already taking a cue from British writers. Scott's *Waverly*, published in 1814, not only initiated an enormous American readership for Scott but began the vogue for American imitations of that writer's historical fictions. Cooper's *The Spy* appeared the same year seventeen-year-old Hawthorne wrote his mother. But though Cooper declared that the growth of American literature required an international copyright agreement,[8] his own independent income enabled him to dictate terms to publishers. When Hawthorne wrote his mother he might have just seen *The Sketch Book,* out in 1820.[9] A story like "The Legend of Sleepy Hollow" applied a Gothic quality to American legend – which was what Hawthorne set himself to do in "Young Goodman Brown." But Irving's start also had been made possible because of family money. *The Sketch Book* was first published in England and its fame traveled across the Atlantic as though he were an English writer.

Hawthorne was poor. The widowed Mrs. Hawthorne was obliged to her brother for her son's college fees and the would-be writer moved back in with her after college because he had no income. How to remove the devil's curse on writing? American magazines and annuals like *The Token* presented a new market only just beginning its phenomenal expansion; many were short-lived, and Hawthorne learned what it felt like to wait in vain for payment or even publication. Goodrich was more competent than most, but there was no reason to be grateful to him, as Bridge reminded Hawthorne when he proposed to dedicate *Twice-Told Tales* to the publisher.[10] *The Token* had paid $108 for eight tales in 1837.[11]

Nevertheless, the possibility of entry into the literary market via the periodicals existed. Another poor man, Poe, was making the effort not to rival the massive English realist novel or Scott's romantic historical one, but to furnish short tales in genres demanded by the magazines. Poe was less interested in American folk traditions than Irving; he was the master of the tale of unlocalized gothic fantasy of a sort to appeal to Hawthorne when he was not nationalistically historical or geographical – in stories like ''The Birthmark'' or ''Rappaccini's Daughter.'' More relevant to Hawthorne's efforts, however, was Poe's aesthetic of brevity. Poe would never write a long novel, and for this never thought to apologize. But his principles of composition, didactically expressed as though they bore no relation to publishing conditions, should be understood as a response to his practical situation. In the face of the popularity of novels Poe insisted on the supremacy of the short tale when he reviewed *Twice-Told Tales* in 1842 in *Graham's Magazine*. In this magazine, of which he was editor, he published, that same year, ''The Masque of the Red Death,'' ''Murders in the Rue Morgue,'' and – expounding his critical theories more fully – ''The Philosophy of Composition.'' He began his note on Hawthorne with the declaration, ''We have always regarded the *Tale* (using this word in its popular acceptation) as affording the best prose opportunity for display of the highest talent. It has peculiar advantages which the novel does not admit. It is, of course, a far fairer field than the essay. It has even points of superiority over the poem.''

Reflecting on the example before him, he declared: "With rare exception – in the case of Mr. Irving's 'Tales of a Traveller' and a few other works of like cast – we have had no American tales of high merit." He had seen "no prose composition by any American which can compare with *some* of [Hawthorne's] articles." A subsequent review elaborated the editor's view that "the tale proper . . . affords unquestionably the fairest field for the exercise of the loftiest talent, which can be afforded by the wide domains of mere prose," and commented in detail on the stories in Hawthorne's book, as all "without exception . . . beautiful," and "belong[ing] to the highest region of Art – an Art subservient to Genius of a very lofty order."[12]

The off-putting title, *Twice-Told Tales,* suggested the author was weary of his productions (the collection might have been retitled "Thrice-Told Tales," after it appeared in a second edition, Poe pointed out), but almost immediately he was recognized as a peer not only by Poe but by Longfellow, who called him a "star . . . newly risen" in the literary heavens of America.[13] *Mosses from an Old Manse* occasioned the most famous "shock of recognition" in the history of American literature, Herman Melville's "Hawthorne and his Mosses," published in the *Literary World* in 1850. There would seem to have been a concerted effort on the part of some literary persons to bring Hawthorne out of the shadows, and Jane Tompkins has recently argued that this even amounted to an "old boy" conspiracy to canonize a male author rather than his female rivals.[14] It is certainly true that Longfellow was a friend of college days and Hawthorne had perhaps even solicited his help.

But Hawthorne's early reviewers were not exclusively male. *Twice-Told Tales* was also launched with help from the two foremost female intellectuals in New England, Elizabeth Palmer Peabody, his Salem neighbor, and Margaret Fuller. Peabody not only introduced him to her sister Sophia, who became his wife in 1839, but as a friend of Emerson and the future publisher of the *Dial* she used her influence in the transcendental establishment to promote his career. She persuaded the historian George Bancroft, Collector of the Port in Boston and the spoils captain of the Democratic Party, to get him his job in the Boston Custom House. Peabody understood Hawthorne's precarious economic position; his impending marriage made it no longer possible to hide out, rent-free, in his mother's house. Personal friendship aside, however, Peabody's review was one in which appreciation for Hawthorne's genius was combined with sympathy for his predicament as a struggling writer. She took note of the peculiar pressures suffered by *male* writers in America in 1841: "In this country, the state of things is so peculiarly unfavorable to that quiet brooding of the spirit over the dark waters, which must precede the utterance of a word of power; – our young men are so generally forced into the arena of business or politics before they have ever discriminated the spirit that they are, from the formless abyss in which they are, that it argues a genius of high order to soar over the roaring gulf of transition in which the elements of society are boiling, into the still heaven of beauty.... One of these true priests is the sweet story-teller, with the flowery name."[15]

Margaret Fuller reviewed both *Twice-Told Tales* and *Mosses from an Old Manse,* the second with somewhat stronger enthusiasm than the first, as she, too, was roused to consider the writer's American handicap and to identify it with the still infantile state of the publishing industry: "Though Hawthorne has now a standard reputation, both for the qualities we have mentioned and the beauty of the style in which they are embodied, yet we believe he has not been very widely read. This is only because his works have not been published in the way to insure extensive circulation in this new, hurrying world of ours. The immense extent of country over which the reading (still very small in proportion to the mere working) community is scattered, the rushing and pushing of our life at this electrical stage of development, leaves no work a chance to be speedily and largely known that is not trumpeted and placarded. And, odious as are the features of a forced and artificial circulation, it must be considered that it does no harm in the end. Bad books will not be read if they are bought instead of good, while the good have no abiding life in the log-cabin settlements and Red River steamboat landings, to which they would in no other way penetrate. Under the auspices of Wiley and Putnam, Hawthorne will have a chance to collect all his own public about him, and that be felt as a presence which before was only a rumor."[16]

Hawthorne had been brought to the attention of the prominent publisher she mentions by an advocate more influential than these elite literary voices. E. A. Duyckinck, editor of the magazine *Arcturus* and later of the *Literary World,* convinced Wiley and Putnam to undertake a library of American authors to rival their series of British writers and to include Hawthorne's *Mosses.* Duyckinck, too, took up the theme of the need for greater recognition of native genius, and in his own review of Hawthorne's early work in 1841, wrote: "Of the American writers destined to live, he is the most original, the one least indebted to foreign models or literary precedents of any kind," but added, "and as the reward of his genius he is the least known to the public. It might be thought that in the small band of true native authors there would be none neglected; that here among a people tenacious of national character, the reputation of the author would be secure; that out of a nation of readers, originality and genius would call forth numerous friends and devotees; that if the authors of the country were few, 'the fewer men, the greater share of honor.' But it is not so, reputation is dependent upon other qualities than worth alone, or we would not have at this day material for an article on the genius of Hawthorne."[17]

The growth of a new, more competitive publishing industry, determined to make use of native authors, turned Hawthorne's fortunes. James T. Fields of Boston became the publisher patron of such writers as Whittier, Holmes, and Longfellow, as well as of Hawthorne. He spotted Hawthorne as a writer whose works would sell at a moment when Hawthorne was receiving widespread publicity and sympathetic interest because he had been summarily fired from a second government job in the Custom House in Salem. Appointed through the influence of Democratic friends, Hawthorne was ousted when the Whigs put Zachary Taylor into the White House; the event seemed a flagrant illustration of the abuses of the spoils system. The brouhaha that resulted when influential literary friends like Longfellow and Lowell protested brought the publisher down to Salem to discover if the castaway had something on his desk that could be published at once.[18]

Fields was a master promoter of books, and he saw that Hawthorne's plan of still another collection, to be entitled "Old Time

Legends; Together with Sketches, Experimental and Ideal," fell below his opportunity. *The Scarlet Letter* may have been conceived by its author as a "tale of the Puritans" like the already published "Endicott and the Red Cross," "The Gentle Boy," or "Young Goodman Brown." Hardly thinking in new terms of this more ambitious work of fiction (not very thick compared to the English "three-decker" of the day), Hawthorne at first thought of packaging it with "several shorter tales and sketches" (156). But Fields saw that it should be issued alone as a book, thickened a bit with an autobiographical preface which would capitalize on the publicity resulting from his expulsion from the Custom House.

The success of *The Scarlet Letter* was immediate, though it never earned its author the kind of money an English writer like Dickens or some of Hawthorne's popular contemporaries in America were making.[19] His tales could now expect a somewhat wider audience; Fields reissued Hawthorne's two published collections in enlarged editions and published nearly all the old tales still uncollected in the final *Snow Image* volume. But turning back to literature as a way of earning a living, Hawthorne still had reason for pessimism. The last sentence of "The Custom House" refers to a minor sketch in *Twice-Told Tales* comically narrated by the Salem water pump, "cup-bearer to the parched populace" (308). The writer, who hopes, desperately, that he will be remembered for something other than this mild temperance fantasy, fears that he may only be re-called by future generations when some antiquary "will point to the locality of THE TOWN PUMP!" If Hawthorne was not ironic in this statement it suggests at least a further complexity in his ambitions and his relation to the market rivalry of short fictions with novels. It was plain that there were a number of different markets for literature.

Currently dominating the field were the female writers, responding to a vast new readership of middle-class women. Precisely when *The Scarlet Letter* made its appearance in the 1850s Susan Warner, Harriet Beecher Stowe, and Maria Cummins published books that would far outsell it. They were part of "the damned mob of scribbling women,"[20] as Hawthorne nastily called them, who became more successful, by mid-century, than most of their male rivals. In recent years this literature has come into its own as another "American Renaissance" with a distinct literary character – a literature responsive to the domestic world of women and to genuine concerns that expressed themselves in plots once thought to be merely sentimental clichés.[21] Whatever their literary virtues, the formulae of the female-authored sentimental novels were, in 1850, a key to popularity. This is probably why, as Tompkins suggests, Hawthorne's next novel, the one he and his wife both liked best of all his novels, was more successful with the public than *The Scarlet Letter,* which gave her a headache. Despite the evidence of Hawthorne's continued preoccupation with the Puritan past and its relation to later American history, *Seven Gables* comes closer to being a sentimental novel than any of his others. With its virgin heroine who is a homemaking paragon and its happy marriage closure in which male aggression is tamed, it was clearly written with the competition in mind.

Hawthorne himself declared in 1851 that *The House of the Seven Gables* was "more proper and natural for me to write, than 'The Scarlet Letter,' " though he may not have been as sure of this identification with the viewpoint of Sophia and other women readers as this sounds, for Sophia, writing rapturously to her sister about the new book which was "totally different from the 'Scarlet Letter,' " confessed, "For himself, he is tired to death of the book. It seems to him at present perfectly inane."[22] But female interests, spelled out in sentimental, domestic themes, already dominated the gift books and periodicals women were reading and for which women writers were writing when he began to place his own short stories and sketches. Such writers as Lydia Sigourney, Catherine Sedgwick, and Sarah Hale were prolific contributors to annuals with parlor-table names like *The Casket, The Gem, The Amulet, Friendship's Offering,* and *Pearls of the West,* as well as *The Token.* And though Hawthorne might sneer at these writers, he was attuned to their mode from the start. Some of his early productions were not so very different from those of his female competitors. This side of his output most pleased some first reviewers. Elizabeth Peabody liked the restricted vision of certain pieces, their confinement to home and hearth, their exclusion of the usual male preoccupations. She praised the "quietness – the apparent leisure, with which he lingers around the smallest point of fact, and unfolds therefrom a world of thought, just as if nothing else existed in the outward universe but that of which he is speaking. The hurried manner that seems to have become the American habit – the spirit of the steam-engine and railroad, has never entered into him."[23] What she identified in this way is a feminine vision. She singled out for praise in *Twice-Told Tales* "Sunday at Home," "Sights from a Steeple," "Little Annie's Ramble," "David Swan," and the most popular of all, "A Rill from the Town Pump." That this last was so popular with the female reader is not surprising; women were always at the forefront of the temperance movement.

There were, Peabody recognized less warmly, stories of another kind in the collection – "The Gray Champion," "The Maypole of Merry Mount," "The Great Carbuncle," and "The Gentle Boy," where Hawthorne showed another intention in his response to the American landscape and to the country's early history. And there were some she disliked. The somber "The Prophetic Pictures" represented the writer's interest in "subjects . . . dangerous to his genius. . . . First-rate genius should leave the odd and peculiar, and especially the fantastic and horrible, to the inferior talent which is obliged to make up its own deficiency by the striking nature of the subject matter."[24] If she rejected this story, which modern readers tend to find fascinating, she did not even mention the mysterious "The Hollow of the Three Hills" or "The Minister's Black Veil," which have also appealed to later readers.

The feminist Margaret Fuller, perhaps a model for Hawthorne's ambiguous Zenobia in *The Blithedale Romance,* made a similar discrimination when reviewing *Mosses from an Old Manse:* "It is in the studies of familiar life that there is most success. In the mere imaginative pieces, the invention is not clearly woven, far from being all compact, and seems a phantom or shadow, rather than a real growth."[25] There is reason to suppose that Hawthorne's writing, far from seeming masculinist and oppositional, appealed particularly to feminine readers and even influenced the writing of women – as well as being itself influenced by the tone of female writing in his time. Years later, Rebecca Harding Davis recalled the impact of her youthful reading of Hawthorne's tales, particularly "Little Annie's Ramble," "Sunday at Home," and "A Rill from the Town Pump," and Harriet Beecher Stowe, in her advice to novice women writers, recommended his "Old Apple Dealer" as a model of the treatment of everyday life.[26]

The same preference for Hawthorne's "feminine" side was shown by some of his male reviewers. From *Twice-Told Tales* Lewis Gaylord Clark chose "Sunday at Home," "A Rill from the Town Pump," "Mr. Higginbotham's Catastrophe," "The Gentle Boy," "Little Annie's Ramble," and "Sights from a Steeple" over "The Minister's Black Veil" and "The Prophetic Pictures."[27] Longfellow's list of favorites was almost the same. He spoke for and to female readers when he said that Hawthorne's "genius is characterized by a large proportion of feminine elements, depth and tenderness of feeling, exceeding purity of mind, and a certain airy grace and arch vivacity in narrating incidents and delineating characters." "The Gentle Boy" was marked by "the strength and beauty of a mother's love," and "Little Annie's Ramble" showed "womanly knowledge of a child's mind and character." "Every woman owes him a debt of gratitude for these lovely visions of womanly faith, tenderness and truth," Longfellow declared. He himself enjoyed best, he said, the times when Hawthorne gave his reader a "pleasant smile" rather than those occasions when he "glares wildly at you, with a strange and painful expression."[28] Some reviewers began to see a double-gendered Hawthorne in the tales. "The perfectness of his style, the completeness of form, the unity of his subject and of all his subjects are masculine: the light play of fancy, the sentiment, are feminine," Duyckinck wrote in 1845.[29] But seeing Hawthorne's principal talent as that of another Fireside Poet – like Longfellow himself – stirred the misgivings of Park Benjamin who felt that the true masculine tone was lacking in American culture.[30]

The question of Hawthorne's relation to the feminine viewpoint and language, to feminine literary form, which he both resented and incorporated, has become more interesting in our own time in the light of feminist revisions of literary history. Those tales of Hawthorne which Melville called "black" often seem to bespeak a hostility to the feminine, a desire to write masculine will on the feminine body, as literalized in the very fables themselves of "The Birthmark" or "Rappaccini's Daughter," both anticipations of *The*

Scarlet Letter, in which the social will of a patriarchal society inscribes its word on the sensuous breast of a woman. Judith Fryer and Judith Fetterley have strongly argued that Hawthorne's female figures are male formulations expressing a masculine view of a dichotomous sexual world, and that his strong female figures are punished for challenging that view. His angelic, submissive women, on the other hand, are actually extinguished, as Fetterly has argued in her analysis of "The Birthmark," or as Sandra Gilbert and Susan Gubar claim in their discussion of "The Snow Image."[31] And perhaps Hawthorne's effort to *rewrite* feminine sentimental modes expresses not only a desire for sexual dominion but, though he might deny any desire to follow their lead, an embittered resolution to recapture the commercial prominence women writers of fiction seemed about to seize from men.[32]

But Hawthorne's feminine empathy, his rivalrous *identification* with women, evident in those sketches and lighter stories that so pleased his contemporaries, are also expressed in the censure of male dominion his sterner tales often exhibit. A woman is almost always *wronged* by Hawthorne's male egomaniacs or idealists like Ethan Brand, Giovanni Guasconti, Parson Hooper, Aylmer. Nina Baym may be right in thinking of Hawthorne as even a male feminist.[33] Whether or not his convictions were wholeheartedly feminist, his authorial mode was that of the feminized male author who knows he has entered a female world in becoming a writer rather than a businessman or politician. Peabody had observed that the young man with literary ambitions would find himself "forced into the arena of business or politics"; Hawthorne's career later prompted Henry James to reflect: "It is not too much to say that even in the present day it is a considerable discomfort in the United States not to be 'in business.' The young man who attempts to launch himself in a career that does not belong to the so-called practical order; the young man who has not, in a word, an office in the business-quarter of the town, with his name painted on the door, has but a limited place in the social system, finds no particular bough to perch upon."[34] Thus, as Baym has argued, writing in nineteenth-century America established itself "as a woman's profession and reading as a woman's avocation."[35] The persona

Hawthorne puts forward as his spokesman, the thoughtful gentleman who evades the alternative world of male action, may signify the triumph of a feminized fictional poetics.[36]

The attention given by his contemporaries to most of Hawthorne's sketches, in which this persona is most prominent, often exceeded that given to *any* – not merely the darker – of his tales. Though Longfellow said that the story "The Great Carbuncle" was his favorite, he quoted most of "Sunday at Home" and all of "A Rill from the Town Pump" in his review. The sketch, Irving's example seemed to show, was not an inferior mode, and the distinction between the sketch and the tale did not seem important. Hawthorne devoted much effort to his sketches, and published them in a quantity equal to his tales; modern critics generally classify only about half of Hawthorne's short writings as "stories" with plot in the Aristotelian sense.[37] Misleadingly, the title *Twice-Told Tales* suggested that Hawthorne's first collection included no other kinds of compositions. Yet the division is evident, and persists, with borderline examples, in *Mosses from an Old Manse* and *The Snow Image and Other Twice-Told Tales*, the latter title again subsuming all its contents as "tales." The *Mosses* preface was really another sketch, "The Old Manse," whose form, ambiguously both autobiographical and fictional, is finally and most complexly exploited in "The Custom House" prefacing *The Scarlet Letter*. Hawthorne anticipated with some accuracy that this extended sketch "would be more widely attractive than the main narrative," which "lacks sunshine."[38]

Hawthorne's first readers may have felt more comfortable with the narrator who made himself so accessible in the sketches in contrast to the puzzling, sardonic mind hidden in some of the tales amd a few gloomy mood pieces like "The Haunted Mind," in which one may read that "in the depths of every heart there is a tomb and a dungeon, though the lights, the music, and revelry above may cause us to forget their existence, and the buried ones, or prisoners whom they hide" (201–2). Most of the sketches are familiar essays that mediate between the reader and the tales, with their oblique imaginative messages. By tone, by implied attitudes, the first person speaker satisfies the Victorian reader's conception of the man of letters, with the "Hawthorne at Home" readers liked to imagine. Hawthorne warned ineffectually that this surrogate was a fiction. He explained in the preface to the third edition of *Twice-Told Tales* that the sketches had not been "the talk of a secluded man with his own mind and heart, (had it been so, they could hardly have failed to be more deeply and permanently valuable,) but the attempts, and very imperfectly successful ones, to open an intercourse with the world" (1152).

He had also warned, in the preface to *Mosses from an Old Manse,* "So far as I am a man of really individual attributes, I veil my face, nor am I, nor have ever been, one of those supremely hospitable people, who serve up their own hearts delicately fried, with brain-sauce, as a titbit for their beloved public" (1147). When he wrote the *Twice-Told Tales* preface he realized the effect he had produced, admitting that "on the internal evidence of his sketches [he had] come to be regarded as a mild, shy, gentle, melancholic, exceedingly sensitive, and not very forcible man, hiding his blushes under an assumed name, the quaintness of which was supposed, somehow or other, to symbolize his personal and literary traits."[39] He added, with a striking self-consciousness about the way an implied author is planted in a text, "He is by no means certain, that some of his subsequent productions have not been influenced and modified by a natural desire to fill up so amiable an outline" (1153).

Poe and Melville both commented on the discrepancy between the "Elia-ish" Hawthorne (as Henry T. Tuckerman called him, referring to Charles Lamb's "Elia") and another Hawthorne altogether. Unlike most reviewers, they thrilled to this other. Poe wrote, " 'The Rill from the Town Pump' which through the *ad captandum* nature of its title has attracted more of public notice than any one other of Mr. Hawthorne's composition, is perhaps, the *least* meritorious." He praised, from *Twice-Told Tales,* "The Hollow of the Three Hills," "The Minister's Black Veil," and "Wakefield," dismissing the usual favorites as *mere* essays lacking "precision and finish."[40] Melville's rhapsodic greeting contained, in addition to warm appreciation of the "sweet Man of Mosses" who had produced the sketch, "Buds and Bird-voices," the warning, "It is the least part of his genius that attracts admiration. Where Hawthorne is known, he seems to be deemed a pleasant writer with a pleasant style, – a sequestered, harmless man, from whom any deep and weighty thing would hardly be anticipated – a man who means no meanings. . . . But in spite of all the Indian-summer sunlight on the hither side of Hawthorne's soul, the other side – like the dark side of the physical sphere – is shrouded in blackness. . . . The world is mistaken in this Nathaniel Hawthorne." He chose a modern favorite, "Young Goodman Brown," as an illustration of the "blackness" he discerned. From its title, he noted, "you would of course suppose that it was a simple little tale, intended as a supplement to 'Goody Two Shoes.' Whereas it is as deep as Dante."[41]

On what principle – of his own artistic evaluation or his expectations of audience appeal – did Hawthorne assemble the published book collections? Did he merely want to achieve a careful balance between the soothing and the troubling? Some of his "blackest" or most mysterious productions were held back longest, though they had been written and published in the magazines earliest. "Roger Malvin's Burial," "Young Goodman Brown," and "My Kinsman, Major Molineux," much esteemed now, may all three have been in manuscript as early as 1828 or 1829, intended for the aborted "Provincial Tales." The first and last appeared in *The Token* in 1831, and the second in a magazine in 1835. But both "Roger Malvin's Burial" and "Young Goodman Brown" were passed over for *Twice-Told Tales*, being reprinted in the *Mosses* volume in 1846; "My Kinsman, Major Molineux" had to wait to be republished until *The Snow Image* collection in 1852. The delay in bringing these to light again does not mean, however, that the writer rejected their mode and mood. Other dark tales were written late – "Rappaccini's Daughter," in *Mosses,* for example, "Ethan Brand" in the last collection. Still, it is "The Snow Image," that gentle little allegory of art which is so much less disturbing than Hawthorne's others on the theme of the artist,[42] which is featured in the title of the last of Hawthorne's "story books."

Whichever one preferred, the fact that there *were* two Hawthornes to be found in these writings – the agreeable, domestic, "feminine" speaker of most of the sketches and the lighter stories and the sardonic mind behind the dark tales – seemed to his contemporaries not only a literary but a personal mystery. For a long time Hawthorne's divided art was discussed in biographic terms rather than in terms of the conflicted literary market he was trying to enter. Tradition identified not only the genteel man of letters known to acquaintances and visible in the social tone of his writing, but a hidden man who expressed himself in the covert messages of more unsettling fiction. There had been the melancholy youthful recluse about whom stories were told, the morbid loner who vanished from view upon his marriage. Hawthorne's career began in a household in which each member ate privately. The young writer's meals were set down on a tray outside his locked door and he was reputed to have seldom ventured outdoors except for solitary walks after nightfall. In a famous letter written before his marriage, he told Sophia about his "solitary years" and the "haunted chamber" where "his lonely youth was wasted." He described himself similarly in his own private journals, and in a letter to Longfellow remembered that "sometimes, through a peephole [he had] caught a glimpse of the real world."[43]

Although writers do, in some sense, speak out of the personal, however much depersonalized, Hawthorne's case is a classic illustration of how unreliably such an identification can be made. Those who disliked his writings linked the legend of his early years to the morbidness or remoteness they perceived in them. His stories expressed no interest in the outside world because the man had had no such interest. Thus Henry A. Beers, in 1895: "The Twice-Told Tales are the work of a recluse, who makes guesses at life from a knowledge of his own heart, acquired by a habit of introspection, but who has had little contact with men," and consequently, many of his tales "were shadowy, and others were morbid and unwholesome."[44] Or Fred Lewis Pattee, in his influential history of the American short story in 1923: Hawthorne's "brooding years of solitude" produced stories "pale and unreal . . . unworldly even to ghostliness, a weird growth of the darkness."[45] But there were always those who, like Poe and Melville, found profundity in the darker Hawthorne. Early twentieth-century biographers either sympathetically read the man of the lonely chamber into the works, like Newton Arvin,[46] or like Herbert Gorman continued to condemn him for his ignorance of the society he lived in.[47]

Criticism had to adjust to a new biographic picture, however, when, in 1948, Randall Stewart showed that even the youthful story writer had a sufficient if not gregarious social side, that his long rambles into the New England countryside were deliberate excursions of observation, that he had a sense of the gritty reality of politics, being close to politicians, and that he made a serious study of American history, reading original sources out of the colonial and eighteenth-century periods particularly. At almost the same time Hyatt Waggoner made Hawthorne into a neo-conservative of the next century, claiming him as a mainstream Christian rather than a subversive challenger of received ideas, as Melville had seen him.[48] And here was a paradox. To demonstrate Hawthorne's Old Believer orthodoxy, Waggoner had to propose a man who, though he almost never went to church, had written his private religiosity into "intricate tissues of symbolism," and proved his attachment to the norm by the language of the secret, unsocial self.

Had the older image been entirely routed? Stewart commented on Hawthorne's letter to Sophia: "When writing a love letter, a man may be tempted to darken his former years so as to brighten by contrast his present felicity."[49] But in the 1970s a "lost notebook" of Hawthorne's came to light in which the impression that Hawthorne remembered himself as immured in melancholy was confirmed.[50] In any case, was not the former view of a dark Hawthorne after all the truer one in some essential sense? Still unforgettable was D. H. Lawrence's warning – like Melville's earlier one – that "blue-eyed darling Nathaniel knew disagreeable things in his inner soul."[51]

Long before Freud supplied a special language for such things as repression or the unconscious, James had remarked that "the fine thing in Hawthorne is that he cared for the deeper psychology" and that his works offer glimpses of "the whole deep mystery of man's soul and conscience."[52] Long after Freud, Frederick Crews rejected the conformist portrait of Stewart and Waggoner, insisting on the presence of a troubled inner man beneath Hawthorne's bland exterior. Crews interpreted the writer's fictions as expressing this dichotomy: "Hawthorne's balance between confession and evasion is reflected in his style, whose distance and abstraction are often confused with Augustan serenity. The meditative poise, the polite irony, the antitheses, the formal diction, and the continual appeal to the sentiments that are generally shared, all serve to neutralize the dangerous knowledge that lies at the bottom of his plots."[53] Most of the major short stories might be read as illustrations of the duplicity of human nature, its buried history and its suppressed motivations. Later biographers returned, with a more complex idea of the psychological issue, to a view of the "haunted" young Hawthorne – and found this image in his writing.[54]

It now seems evident that, antibiographic as the New Criticism of the 1950s was in intention, its practice of close reading paradoxically tended to promote interpretation of Hawthorne's fiction as a symbolic utterance of the self rather than as open statement and realist presentation. That art is a significant hieroglyphic language of the psyche has been the basic contention of studies of Hawthorne's tales that take their critical premises from psychoanalysis. Crews's readings of the now favored dark tales was a Freudian vision of heroes oppressed, like their author, by fantasies of guilt. James R. Mellow's *Nathaniel Hawthorne and his Times,* published in 1980, is less at pains to discover the relation of Hawthorne's stories to the social world, as suggested in its title, than to study private stresses: "The darker side of Hawthorne's mind seemed reserved for his early tales. The presiding themes there – the secret springs of shame, the hidden nature of guilt, the communion of sinners – speak of the tormented mind. . . . Morality – the codes of a particular society at a particular time – does not become his real province as a writer."[55] Hawthorne's most recent biographer, Edwin Haviland Miller, rejecting the view that Hawthorne was interested in society or theology, insists that he was a private, skeptical person who "never left home," never left the preoccupations of his introverted youth. His writings, says Miller, are best described as he described one of his own late, unfinished romances: "Our story is an internal one, dealing as little as possible with outward events and taking hold of them, only when it cannot be helped, in order by means of them to delineate the history of a mind bewildered in certain errors."[56]

Hawthorne's place among the Most Important American Writers has never been seriously challenged. But it was the long romances, especially *The Scarlet Letter,* that for many years remained conspicuous in literary histories and school reading lists. The short stories and sketches came to seem more negligible. Even F. O. Matthiessen, whose seminal *American Renaissance* initiated, in 1941, an intensive appreciation of Hawthorne's symbolic techniques and moral themes, relied almost exclusively on *The Scarlet Letter* and the longer works that followed it. Already in Hawthorne's lifetime, once he became distinctly visible as a novelist, his stories drew less attention from a public which seemed to like his novels better than he sometimes did himself. The novel was not exactly his metier, he felt. He continued to wish that he could write like the contemporary English realists, and condemned his books for not reflecting common life.[57] But there was enough of the sense of the real – of the past or of his own day – in his novels to satisfy readers who did not look for symbolic design or hidden meanings. The stories, on the other hand, seemed altogether too frequently "allegorical" for the current taste.

He himself was the first to say so. In the small mock preface attached to "Rappaccini's Daughter," the pseudonymous author, M. l'Aubépine, is said to have written previous works, their French titles all translations of Hawthorne's. Ironically, these are multi-volumed novels, not brief tales – *L'Artiste du Beau* – *The Artist of the Beautiful* – is a work in "5 tom," for example. But M. l'Aubépine's "praiseworthy and admirable prolixity" has not, it would appear, attained for him "the brilliant success of Eugene Sue" (976). His deficiencies are those of which Hawthorne always convicted himself – an "inveterate love of allegory" which tended to "steal away the human warmth out of his conceptions" and "a very slight embroidery of outward manners – the faintest possible counterfeit of real life." Poe took the author's cue in his review of *Mosses from an Old Manse,* and identified a cause of Hawthorne's failure of popularity as "the strain of allegory which completely overwhelms the greater number of his subjects, and which in some measure interferes with the direct conduct of absolutely all."[58]

It is not quite clear what Poe – or Hawthorne himself – meant by allegory; it was certainly not a term limited to the representation of abstract ideas in a consistent, continuous symbolic narrative after the style of *Pilgrim's Progress* – a description that applies to only a few of Hawthorne's compositions. But if any suggestion of the nonliteral or symbolic was "allegory," then Hawthorne was, one might say, frequently allegorical. The term was a negative one for the nineteenth-century reader of realist fiction.[59] In *Moby-Dick*, Melville's narrator speaks for the literal reality of the real whale known to the fisheries, fearing that otherwise "landsmen" might take him as "a monstrous fable, or, still worse and more detestable, a hideous and intolerable allegory." But Melville, it should be remembered, was grateful to Hawthorne for having perceived "the part-&-parcel allegoricalness" of his book.[60] It would appear that for Melville and Hawthorne, as for Emerson, allegory was not distinguished from symbolism with any precision; both terms signified those suggestive images of "deeper and unspeakable meanings" that Melville praised in his review of Hawthorne's tales. Yet they also distrusted the "allegorical" impulse. Hawthorne said warily to his publisher in 1854, "I am not quite sure that I entirely comprehend my own meaning in some of these blasted allegories."[61]

The prejudice against this vaguely defined quality continued in subsequent decades to dim interest in Hawthorne's short fiction. Henry Tuckerman wrote in 1870 that Hawthorne's successes were "those in which the human predominates. Ingenuity and moral significance are finely displayed, it is true, in his allegories; but sometimes they are coldly fanciful, and do not win the sympathies as in those instances where the play of the heart relieves the dim workings of the abstract and the supernatural."[62] And James, in the first and still the most influential book-length study of Hawthorne, accepted Hawthorne's own deprecation of his short "trifles." He called "Roger Malvin's Burial," "Rappaccini's Daughter," and "Young Goodman Brown" "little masterpieces" blemished by their "metaphysical" or "allegorical" design. Following Poe, James declared that, to his own mind also, allegory "is quite one of the lighter exercises of the imagination. . . . It is apt to spoil two things – a story and a moral, a meaning and a form; and the taste for it is responsible for a large part of the forcible-feeble writing that has been inflicted upon the world."[63]

It was a judgment that persisted. Nearly forty years later, W. C. Brownell, who had been Henry James's editor, called Hawthorne "allegory mad."[64] When the New Criticism identified symbolism as the chief feature of poetry and deprecated the fixed one-to-one correspondence of "idea" and "thing" in traditional allegory, this dismissal of Hawthorne was taken up again on more precisely defined grounds. Charles Feidelson, finding poetic symbolism to be the great literary breakthrough of the 1850s, ranked Hawthorne below Melville because he had, Feidelson felt, clung to allegory – except that he was frequently "a symbolist in spite of himself."[65] But with its preference for close readings of limited texts – short poems or stories – modern formalist criticism also rediscovered some of the virtues of unity of effect Poe had found in Hawthorne's tales. Despite the objection to his supposed "allegory," Hawthorne became the subject of studies concentrating on imagery and the tensions of language. The notorious ambiguity which had formerly put off the readers of his more baffling stories now seemed analogous to the rich multiplicity of verbal suggestion in poetry.

Hawthorne, the allegorist-symbolist, could now be seen as a case of what Richard Harter Fogle called "the light and the dark" – clarity of design combined with subtle ambiguity of meaning through imagery – and Fogle paid as much loving attention to such stories as "The Minister's Black Veil," "Young Goodman Brown," and "Ethan Brand" as to each of the long fictions.[66] Q. D. Leavis's important essay of 1951, "Hawthorne as Poet," maintained that the "essential Hawthorne" was the author of *The Scarlet Letter, The Blithedale Romance,* and such stories as "Young Goodman Brown," "The Maypole of Merry Mount," "My Kinsman, Major Molineux," and other stories and sketches associated with them – all works, she felt, whose language is, like Shakespeare's, "symbolic, and richly so."[67] At the same time, a Hawthorne whose main virtues were formal repelled Yvor Winters. He called the stories "slight performances" that either "lack meaning . . . or they lack reality of embodiment . . . or having a measure of both, they seem incapable of justifying the intensity of method"[68] – a judgment that seemed a return to the response to Hawthorne's "allegory" made by his first critics and by James.

What early critics and James deplored as the aesthetic trifling of allegory and the New Criticism was ready to admire as ambiguity and multiple meaning – and Winters to deprecate as obscurantism – made Hawthorne's tales, some decades later, seem apt examples

24

for deconstructionist interpretation. The way Hawthorne's stor[ies] and novels often refuse to close on a clear meaning invited the conclusion that his subject was really the futility of expecting that final meaning can be found. His method of "alternative possibilities," which irritated Winters, might be viewed as the fruit of a basic skepticism. Kenneth Dauber observes that there are two irreconcilable stories in "Rappaccini's Daughter" – not ambiguity but two clarities which subsist independently of each other. The purpose of l'Aubépine, Hawthorne's fictional author, is, he thinks, "the elimination of purpose . . . the attempt, by authorially affirming opposite interpretations of the same fiction, by linking in a single printed text two contradictory stories, to create a fiction that affirms itself."[69] J. Hillis Miller reads James's remark that in Hawthorne, "when the image becomes importunate it is in danger of seeming to stand for nothing more serious than itself," as a comment on Hawthorne's self-reflexive irony. Hawthorne's constantly expressed complaint that he had failed to communicate himself seems to this critic an admission of the "incommunicability of selfhood," and he finds this theme central to such stories as "Wakefield," "The Christmas Banquet," and above all, "The Minister's Black Veil." When Hawthorne says, in the preface to *Twice-Told Tales*, that his pages, if looked at in the sun, may turn out to be blank, he may be suggesting the futility of the expectation of referential meaning. "The Minister's Black Veil" appropriately chooses, says Miller, the form of parable, which promises a revelation or illumination but also withholds it. "The veil is the type and symbol of the fact that all signs are potentially unreadable, or that the reading of them is potentially unverifiable."[70]

But the judgment has predominated that Hawthorne stories are *about* something other than their own status as language. James initiated the skeptical aesthetic approach to Hawthorne's Puritan subject matter. Melville discerned in the tales a "blackness, ten times black," and "whether [Hawthorne] has simply availed himself of this mystical blackness as a means to the wondrous effects he makes it produce in his lights and shades; or whether there really lurks in him, perhaps unknown to himself, a touch of Puritanic gloom," he confessed he could not tell. In either case, Hawthorne's "power of blackness derives its force from its appeals to

sense of Innate Depravity and Original Sin, from
_s, in some shape or other, no deeply thinking mind
/holly free."[71] James also saw the Puritan element
but was in no doubt that in stories like "Young
_vn" it was no more than an aesthetic device: "The
ral sense, the consciousness of sin and hell, of the
fearful nature of our responsibilities and the savage character of
our Taskmaster – these things had been lodged in the mind of a
man of Fancy, whose fancy had straightway begun to take liberties
and play tricks with them – to judge them (Heaven forgive him!)
from the poetic and aesthetic point of view, the point of view of
entertainment and irony."[72]

James's view was borrowed too exactly by Van Wyck Brooks:
"The Puritan conscience in Hawthorne is like some useful Roman
vessel of glass which has been buried for centuries in the earth
and comes forth at last fragile as a dragon-fly's wing, shot through
with all the most exquisite colors. . . . Could anything be more exquisite? could anything more utterly fail to connect with reality
in a practical Yankee world?"[73] Yet there were always others who
insisted on the genuine vitality of Hawthorne's interest in Puritanism. Paul Elmer More believed that his ancestral religion had
reasserted itself in Hawthorne, coloring his personal view of himself and his society,[74] and, in 1934, in the Hawthorne volume of
the influential "American Writers Series," Austin Warren claimed
Hawthorne as a self-conscious latter-day Calvinist.[75] Hawthorne
himself said, in the preface to *The Scarlet Letter*, that even if his
Puritan ancestors might scorn him, "strong traits of their nature
have intertwined themselves" with his own (127).

This statement, as well as Melville's remarks, hints at one solution to the question of Hawthorne's Puritanism. The nineteenth-
century man could not have been a literal believer in the theology
of seventeenth-century Puritanism. He believed in Puritanism *in
a sense.* Symbol readers and psychological critics seized the idea
that Hawthorne had used the ancestral religion to express his in-
tuitions about human nature, its ineradicable propensity to evil
and hypocrisy, and the sense of guilt that may plague the most
noble. Hawthorne was not, according to this view, so much in-

terested in the beliefs of the Puritans as in how they might parallel later ideas. Harry Levin, in his book which borrowed its title from Melville, *The Power of Blackness,* summarized the view that "Hawthorne remained a Calvinist in psychology if not in theology."[76]

That Hawthorne's writings have social and moral convictions at their core is a conclusion that close reading of symbolic design could support rather than dissipate. Waggoner, as noted, and Roy R. Male[77] argued for a Christian humanism discernible in patterns of traditional symbols. The influence not only of Freud, but also of Jung, who posited the existence of a "collective unconscious," produced a criticism that, still using a formalist method, sought out archetypal myths and typologies in Hawthorne's fiction. William Bysshe Stein's *Hawthorne's Faust: A Study of the Devil Archetype,* for example, detected an ancient archetype in the symbolic patterns of Hawthorne's tales.[78] But the permanent patterns of human experience are not the shapes of exact history. For these critics, "history as history had little meaning for Hawthorne artistically," as Seymour Gross wrote.[79] What interested Hawthorne, they felt, was a universal human constant.

But myth, after all, may be only history generalized – and no history was more significantly in the process of being made into myth in Hawthorne's time than that of America itself. Roy Harvey Pearce, summarizing on the occasion of Hawthorne's Centenary in 1964, called for a change of view: "In our time, the image of Hawthorne as symbolic romancer has been marvelously elucidated, verified, and expounded.... We have allegorized, mythologized, psychoanalyzed, theologized – all to the end of deriving Hawthorne's symbols from a world which neither he nor we ever could have made.... Hawthorne is the symbolist as historian. And as such, he derives his symbols not from myth or exotic learning or Swedenborgianism, or post-Kantianism, but from the facts of history itself – the factuality of American historical experience as he studied and understood it."[80] Q. D. Leavis had not stopped at pointing out formal beauties in Hawthorne's tales. Her essay – which initiated a recognition of the importance of "My Kinsman, Major Molineux" – challenged the view that Hawthorne was uninterested in his society and its origins. His greatest works,

like this story, she insisted, expressed his "sense of being part
of the contemporary America [by means of] a concern for its
evolution."[81]

One interest Hawthorne always had for some academic spe-
cialists, those who modestly preferred to call themselves scholars
rather than critics, was prompted by the undeniable historical element in many of his tales. Whatever the New Critics thought about
the relevance of history, Hawthorne himself was interested in the
New England past, deliberately studied it and mined it for his
writing. But whereas an older historicism merely pointed out his
sources in historical reading, the centrality of history to his imaginative effort has more recently been urged. Michael Davitt Bell
begins his *Hawthorne and the Historical Romance of New England*
with the declaration, "Nathaniel Hawthorne was one of the most
historically minded of our major novelists."[82] Asking whether
Hawthorne was a Puritan, Bell remarks, is a little like asking
whether a child psychologist is a child. Most recently, Michael J.
Colacurcio has elaborated the case not so much for Hawthorne's
personal religious faith as for his lifelong effort, initiated in the
early tales, "to discover the moral significance of America's Puritan
exceptionalism." For Colacurcio, Hawthorne's "sense of depravity –
his power of blackness – is rightly apprehended only as a consciously historical re-cognition of the Puritan 'Way' in which
America had begun." The chief aim of the young Hawthorne,
forced to give up his early projects of books of connected tales
suggestively titled "Seven Tales of My Native Land," "Provincial
Tales," or the four "Legends of the Province House" as well as in
the conception that originally embraced *The Scarlet Letter* and other
stories of the New England past, was nothing other than this.[83]

Not surprisingly, the stories that have chiefly interested the critics
who have contributed to this volume are among those which criticism has for some time now found most fascinating and challenging although they were not the favorites of Hawthorne's
contemporary readers. Each has received every kind of critical
attention – the close reading for verbal nuance and structure of
formalist criticism, criticism motivated by an interest in genres and
literary tradition or the traditions of mythology or religion or an

interest in the history of intellectual ideas or cultural concepts, or biographical criticism, psychological criticism, feminist criticism, or criticism preoccupied with the study of backgrounds and sources, or criticism evolving from a conviction of the importance of history as a key to the meaning of literature as well as criticism denying that importance, and even the antiinterpretive critical approach of deconstruction. The reader of these new essays will be interested to see how five of today's Hawthorne critics employ one or another approach, and sometimes more, to these favorite tales, and how they have located themselves in ongoing discussions that are making new discoveries about the meaning of the stories.

In explaining Hawthorne's early stories – particularly "Young Goodman Brown," "My Kinsman, Major Molineux," and "Roger Malvin's Burial" – as the expression of the writer's historical interest, Michael Colacurcio redefines source study and critiques the antihistorical views represented by psychological and other approaches. David Leverenz traces Hawthorne's mythopoeic adaptation of the figure of Satan and brings allusion and biography as well as the analysis of Hawthorne's own times to bear on a political reading of some of the same stories. Carol Bensick, having illustrated the importance of reader recognition of allusion in Hawthorne's seemingly *un*historical "Rappaccini's Daughter," returns to religious conceptions as a source of interpretation. Edgar Dryden approaches the "The Minister's Black Veil" as an example of the genre of parable and unites an interest in biblical traditions of interpretation with modern hermeneutics. Rita Gollin connects patterns of language and figuration with the psychological and biographical in "Ethan Brand."

NOTES

1 The story of Hawthorne's unsuccessful early attempts to publish a book of stories is given in Nelson Adkins's "The Early Projected Works of Nathaniel Hawthorne," *Papers of the Bibliographical Society of America* 39 (1945), 119–55, and, along with the publishing history of the tales and sketches included in *Twice-Told Tales, Mosses from an Old Manse,* and *The Snow-Image and Other Twice-Told Tales,* in *The Works of Na-*

thaniel Hawthorne, Centenary Edition, ed. William Charvat, Roy Harvey Pearce, Claude M. Simpson, et al. (Columbus, Ohio: Ohio State University Press, 1962–1988), 20 vols., vol. 9, pp. 485–533; 10, pp. 499–537; 11, pp. 379–409. Accounts of Hawthorne's early years are provided in standard biographies: Randall Stewart, *Nathaniel Hawthorne: A Biography* (New Haven: Yale University Press, 1948), James R. Mellow, *Nathaniel Hawthorne and His Times* (Boston: Houghton Mifflin Co., 1980), Arlin Turner, *Nathaniel Hawthorne: A Biography* (New York and Oxford: Oxford University Press, 1980), and Edwin Haviland Miller, *Salem Is My Dwelling Place: A Life of Nathaniel Hawthorne* (Iowa City: University of Iowa Press, 1991).

2 Nathaniel Hawthorne, *Tales and Sketches,* ed. Roy Harvey Pearce (New York: The Library of America, 1982), p. 332. Subsequent references to Hawthorne's tales and sketches will be made to this edition.

3 The reviewer was Park Benjamin, writing in the *American Monthly Magazine,* n.s. vol. 2, October 1836. Reprinted in B. Bernard Cohen, ed., *The Recognition of Nathaniel Hawthorne* (Ann Arbor, Mich.: University of Michigan Press, 1969), p. 5.

4 Nathaniel Hawthorne, *Novels,* ed. Millicent Bell (New York: The Library of America, 1983), p. 127. Subsequent references to Hawthorne's long fictions will be made to this edition.

5 J. Donald Crowley, *Hawthorne: The Critical Heritage* (New York: Barnes & Noble, 1970), p. 141. Poe's essay appeared in *Godey's Lady's Book,* November 1847.

6 For discussion of Hawthorne's sales, see Crowley, pp. 10–13.

7 Letter to Elizabeth Hathorne, March 13, 1821, in *Works,* vol. 15, p. 139. For further discussion of this letter, see essay by David Leverenz in this book.

8 Cooper wrote, "No man will pay a writer, for an epic, a tragedy, a sonnet, a history, or a romance, when he can get a work of equal merit for nothing" (James Fenimore Cooper, *Notions of the Americans* [Albany, N.Y.: State University of New York Press, 1991], p. 347).

9 *The Sketch Book*'s successful combination of stories and sketches had, by the early 1830s, already produced a number of imitations, including Longfellow's *Outre Mer* and collections like Eliza Leslie's *Pencil Sketches,* Lydia Sigourney's *Tales and Essays,* Catherine M. Sedgwick's *Tales and Sketches,* Theodore S. Fay's *Dreams and Reveries of a Quiet Man,* the last title suggesting the special mood that marked such volumes and that Hawthorne might have meant to cast over his own effort of this kind.

10 "I am perfectly aware that he has taken a good deal of interest in you,

but when did he ever do anything for you without a *quid pro quo?*'' Bridge wrote Hawthorne (*Works,* vol. 9, p. 505).

11 *Works,* vol. 9, p. 497.

12 Crowley, pp. 84–5, 88, 91.

13 Crowley, p. 55.

14 Jane Tompkins, *Sensational Designs: The Cultural Work of American Fiction, 1790–1860* (New York and Oxford: Oxford University Press, 1985), pp. 3–39.

15 Albert J. von Frank, *Critical Essays on Hawthorne's Short Stories* (Boston: G. K. Hall, 1991), p. 26. Arlin Turner first identified Peabody's authorship of this review, which was published anonymously in the *New Yorker* in 1838 (*Nathaniel Hawthorne Journal* 4 [1974], 75–82).

16 Von Frank, p. 40.

17 Crowley, pp. 74–5.

18 Richard Brodhead summarizes Field's role in creating the American canon which elevated these writers by means of unprecedented efforts of publicity and distribution. *The School of Hawthorne* (New York and Oxford: Oxford University Press, 1986), pp. 54–8. C. E. Frazer Clark, Jr., has described the publicity Hawthorne received as a result of his firing from the Custom House. ''Posthumous Papers of a Decapitated Surveyor: *The Scarlet Letter* in the Salem Press,'' *Studies in the Novel,* 2 (1970), 395–419.

19 Hawthorne's total income from *Mosses from an Old Manse* for 1851 and 1852 was one hundred and fifty dollars. Even *The Scarlet Letter* earned only fifteen hundred dollars for Hawthorne between 1850 and 1864, selling 13,500 copies as compared to the 800,000 copies of *Pickwick Papers* sold before the expiration of copyright (Crowley, p. 11).

20 Hawthorne letter to William D. Ticknor, January 19, 1855, *Works,* vol. 17, p. 304.

21 See Nina Baym, *Women's Fiction: A Guide to Novels by and about Women in America, 1820–1870* (Ithaca and London: Cornell University Press, 1978); Tompkins, *Sensational Designs.*

22 *Works,* vol. 2, p. xvi; ''Sophia Hawthorne as a Literary Editor and Educator: A Letter,'' ed. N. Luanne Jenkins Hurst, *The Nathaniel Hawthorne Review,* vol. 18, no. 2 (Fall, 1992), 5.

23 Von Frank, p. 28.

24 Von Frank, p. 30.

25 Von Frank, p. 39.

26 Davis, *Bits of Gossip* (Boston: Houghton, Mifflin & Co., 1904) and Stowe, ''How Shall I Learn to Write,'' *Hearth and Home* 1, Jan. 17, 1869, 56–7. Cited by Brodhead, pp. 218, 219.

27 *Works,* vol. 9, p. 507.

28 Crowley, pp. 81–2, 58.

29 Crowley, p. 97.

30 *Works,* vol. 9, p. 509.

31 Judith Fryer, *The Faces of Eve: Women in the Nineteenth Century American Novel* (New York: Oxford University Press, 1976); Judith Fetterley, *The Resisting Reader: A Feminist Approach to American Fiction* (Bloomington: Indiana University Press, 1978). See Fetterley's reading of "The Birthmark," p. 24, and Sandra Gilbert and Susan Gubar's of "The Snow Image," p. 618, in *The Madwoman in the Attic: The Woman Writer and the Nineteenth-Century Literary Imagination* (New Haven and London: Yale University Press, 1979).

32 Hawthorne's famous remark about "scribbling women" made it clear to his publisher in 1855 that he was resolved *not* to compete by imitation, for he went on to say, "I should have no chance of success while the public taste is occupied with their trash – and should be ashamed of myself if I did succeed" (see note 20, above). But it is not at all clear that he had really resisted the temptation so completely, especially at the start of his career.

33 Nina Baym, "Thwarted Nature: Nathaniel Hawthorne as Feminist," in Fritz Fleischmann, ed., *American Novelists Revisited. Essays in Feminist Criticism* (Boston: G. K. Hall, 1982).

34 Henry James, *Literary Criticism* (New York: The Library of America, 1984), p. 342.

35 Nina Baym, *Women's Fiction: A Guide to Novels by and about Women, 1820–1970* (Ithaca: Cornell University Press, 1978), p. 11.

36 The argument for the "feminization of a masculine poetics" in Hawthorne's time has been recently made by Leland S. Person, Jr., *Aesthetic Headaches: Women and Masculine Poetics in Poe, Melville, and Hawthorne* (Athens and London: The University of Georgia Press, 1988), especially Chapter 1.

37 Lea Bertani Vozar Newman, *A Reader's Guide to the Short Stories of Nathaniel Hawthorne* (Boston: G. K. Hall & Co., 1979) treats a list of fifty-four short stories.

38 Crowley, p. 151; and see Crowley, pp. 155, 159, 164–5, for the response of first reviewers.

39 How exactly this was so is shown by the recollection of Henry T. Tuckerman: "I remember, when I first encountered one of his sketches in a Boston annual, I thought Hawthorne was an assumed name quaintly devised for an Elia-ish incognito; and it struck me as quite appropriate, for is not hawthorn the favorite hedge, and is not its very

mention suggestive of verdure, home, and a cheering wayside?'' Crowley, p. 476.

40 Crowley, pp. 85, 88.

41 Crowley, pp. 115–16, 123.

42 For a comparison of ''The Snow Image'' with ''The Prophetic Pictures,'' ''The Artist of the Beautiful,'' and ''Drowne's Wooden Image,'' see Millicent Bell, *Hawthorne's View of the Artist* (Albany, N.Y.: State University of New York Press, 1962).

43 Hawthorne letter to Longfellow, June 4, 1837, *Works,* vol. 15, p. 252.

44 Henry A. Beers, *Initial Studies in American Letters* (New York: The Chatauqua Press, 1895), p. 120. Quoted in von Frank, p. 8.

45 Fred Lewis Pattee, *The Development of the American Short Story* (New York: Harper & Bros., 1923, pp. 91–114). Quoted in von Frank, p. 8.

46 Newton Arvin, *Hawthorne* (Boston: Little, Brown and Co., 1929).

47 Herbert Gorman, *Hawthorne: A Study in Solitude* (New York: George H. Doran Co., 1927).

48 Hyatt H. Waggoner, *Hawthorne* (Cambridge: Harvard University Press, 1955).

49 Stewart, p. 37.

50 It appears that Sophia Hawthorne's transcription of Hawthorne's notebook statement, ''In this dismal chamber FAME was won'' (in *Passages from the American Notebooks* published in 1868) had deleted a word that gave an aspect of even intenser gloom to Hawthorne's recollection. He had written, ''In this dismal and squalid chamber FAME was won.'' *Hawthorne's Lost Notebook, 1835–1841,* ed. Barbara S. Mouffe (University Park, Pa.: Pennsylvania State University Press, 1978), p. 24.

51 D. H. Lawrence, *Studies in Classic American Literature* (New York: Doubleday, 1953), p. 93.

52 James, *Literary Criticism,* p. 368.

53 Frederick Crews, *The Sins of the Fathers* (New York: Oxford University Press, 1966), p. 12.

54 For the most recent psychological study of Hawthorne see Gloria C. Erlich, *Family Themes and Hawthorne's Fiction: The Tenacious Web* (New Brunswick, N.J.: Rutgers University Press, 1984).

55 Mellow, pp. 57–8.

56 Miller, p. xv.

57 As he wrote in ''The Custom House'': ''The wiser effort would have been, to diffuse thought and imagination through the opaque substance of to-day, and thus make it a bright transparency; to spiritualize

the burden that began to weigh so heavily; to seek, resolutely, the true and indestructible value that lay hidden in the petty and wearisome incidents, and ordinary characters, with which I was now conversant" (150–1).

58 Crowley, p. 145.

59 See Nina Baym, *Novels, Readers, and Reviewers: Responses to Fiction in Antebellum America* (Ithaca and London: Cornell University Press, 1984), pp. 91–3.

60 Herman Melville, *Moby-Dick,* ed. Harrison Hayford and Hershel Parker (New York: W. W. Norton, 1967), pp. 177, 568 (letter to Sophia Hawthorne, January 8, 1852).

61 Letter to James T. Fields, April 13, 1854. *Works* vol. 17, p. 201.

62 Crowley, p. 460.

63 James, *Literary Criticism,* p. 366.

64 W. C. Brownell, *American Prose Masters* (London: Smith, Elder, 1909), pp. 63–130.

65 Charles Feidelson, Jr., *Symbolism and American Literature* (Chicago: University of Chicago Press, 1953), pp. 8–9.

66 Richard Harter Fogle, *Hawthorne's Fiction: the Light and the Dark* (Norman, Okla., University of Oklahoma Press, 1952).

67 Von Frank, p. 94. Originally, "Hawthorne as Poet," *Sewanee Review* 59 (1951), 179–205.

68 Yvor Winters, "Maule's Curse, or Hawthorne and the Problem of Allegory," *In Defense of Reason* (New York: W. Morrow, 1947), pp. 157, 174–5.

69 Kenneth Dauber, *Rediscovering Hawthorne* (Princeton, N.J.: Princeton University Press, 1977), pp. 34–5.

70 J. Hillis Miller, *Hawthorne and History: Defacing It* (Cambridge, Mass., and Oxford: Basil Blackwell, 1991), pp. 57, 97.

71 Crowley, pp. 115–16.

72 James, *Literary Criticism,* p. 365.

73 Van Wyck Brooks, *America's Coming of Age* (Garden City, N.Y.: Doubleday, 1958), pp. 35–6.

74 Paul Elmer More, "Hawthorne: Looking Before and After," in *Shelburne Essays,* First Series (Boston: Houghton, Mifflin, 1904). See also the significantly titled essay, "The Solitude of Nathaniel Hawthorne," in the same collection.

75 Austin Warren, Introduction, American Writers Series, *Hawthorne* (New York: American Book Co., 1934).

76 Harry Levin, *The Power of Blackness* (New York: Alfred A. Knopf, 1958), p. 55.

77 Roy R. Male, *Hawthorne's Tragic Vision* (New York, W. W. Norton, 1957).

78 William Bysshe Stein, *Hawthorne's Faust: A Study of the Devil Archetype* (Gainesville: University of Florida, 1953).

79 Seymour Gross, " 'My Kinsman, Major Molineux': History as Moral Adventure," *Nineteenth-Century Fiction*, 12 (1957), 97–109.

80 Roy Harvey Pearce, "Romance and the Study of History," *Hawthorne Centenary Essays* (Columbus, Ohio: Ohio State University Press, 1964), p. 222.

81 Von Frank, p. 95.

82 Michael Davitt Bell, *Hawthorne and the Historical Romance of New England* (Princeton, N.J.: Princeton University Press, 1971), p. vii.

83 Michael J. Colacurcio, *The Province of Piety: Moral History in Hawthorne's Early Tales* (Cambridge: Harvard University Press, 1984), pp. 14, 28.

2

"Certain Circumstances": Hawthorne and the Interest of History

MICHAEL J. COLACURCIO

1

NOTHING would seem more obvious at first glance than the historical dimension of Hawthorne's literary art. His work of widest international reputation, *The Scarlet Letter*, is set squarely in the midst of the "Puritan" seventeenth century, and it shows all the signs of a determined inquiry into the moral circumstances of this relevant and specifiable past. The settings of his tales turn out to be quite various, but from among them a modest number set in colonial New England have attracted a disproportionate share of attention, as if in recognition that such "local history" were somehow his true metier. And compared to the universalism of contemporaries like Emerson and Thoreau, Hawthorne's bookish curiosity about historical particularities would certainly seem a distinguishing mark. So it might appear irresponsible to ignore the problems which arise when our literary present is constituted as an imitation of an historical past: This is now, as always, whenever anyone reads; but that was then. What if it was all different?

At the same time, however, few readers appear to relish the suggestion that what they read as "literature" may require an effort of historical reconstruction – and even of something like research. Perhaps we all begin by defining "the literary" so as to preclude that exact possibility: now for something on my own terms; or else, with a little more finesse, something complete in itself, something which invents and deploys its own world of fact and assumption. Granted, all acts of writing are past to the reader; and the *further* past of historical fiction may well compound the problem of possible human difference. But all acts of reading are present; nor does literature properly speaking occur until someone actually reads. So most readers are inclined to trust their own instincts: That was then, but this is now; and life is short.

Nor have the institutions of academic criticism always opposed these readerly assumptions.[1] True, many Professors of Literature appear duty-bound to lecture their classes on something called background or context; and many of them are known to lament that teaching grows more difficult every year, as each new class seems less well informed about the history of the world where literature has been written and read.[2] But most students prove immune to this preprofessional embarrassment: They have, after all, only so much time for each course; nor did they enroll in "English" with the same factual expectations as in history or sociology. And professors usually concede the point in the end: When the push of class discussion comes to the shove of a take-home paper, any fair comment on theme or style will usually suffice. A more complex approach – more worldly or more "intertextual" – must wait till graduate school. Or for some "New Historicism," to point a way outside the well enclosed garden of literary study.[3]

Meanwhile, of the explicit "approaches" that have retarded the interest of history, one may count the discrediting effect of "source studies." In these, a scholar persuaded of the obvious – that the "Puritanism" of "Young Goodman Brown" or the revolutionary lore of "My Kinsman, Major Molineux" surely implies some special historical knowledge – sets out to locate the very books from which Hawthorne has derived his facts. Such studies have been successful in certifying an impressive number of works Hawthorne *must* have read. Often enough, however, historical consideration ends with the thrill of the discovery, truly electric to the investigator, but hard to communicate to the less fortunate audience. A "fact" is added to the lore of "literary history"; but the avid reader, lured to the library by the promise of insight, almost always asks, "So what?" Or else she or he is soberly instructed that, though Hawthorne has read something which *happened* to spur the creative process, he has of course gone on to "use history" for his own literary end – implying, always, that we need not trouble ourselves much about the issues of the sources themselves.[4] We honor thus the artist's creativity, but we also empower our own autonomous reading. Imagination transmutes every difficulty of worldly fact into the "textual" condition of rhetoric. A most convenient system, truly.

But another form of criticism has also acted to counter the interest of history in Hawthorne – one so habitual as to appear inevitable. Psychology may or may not appear to us as Queen of the Sciences, but whenever we sit down to read for more than mere diversion, we usually find ourselves within its quietly extensive domain; for, as serious readers, we imagine we are looking for insight into something like "the human condition" – glorious or pitiful, yet pretty much unchanged over time. Long since persuaded that the pursuit of wisdom begins nowhere but in self-knowledge, we go on to decide that literature shall be our primary aid to that reflection. Conscientiously secured and arranged by our colleges, the corpus of canonized texts represents, to us, a preserve of all the more important traits of our own curious species. Thus literature continues, without fail, to appear "more philosophical than history": It looks for evidences of things that are *always* true, about ourselves.

In loyalty to this complex of assumptions we steadfastly resist the suggestion that historical change may be real and radical – that "the self" may be largely the creation of modern ideology, and that the notion of an essential human psyche may be only a narcissistic illusion. Accordingly, in the case of Hawthorne, we seize some fragment of his language to insist that his true interest can be nothing but the profounder workings of "our common nature."[5] His characters may be Puritans or other awkward provincials but his real interests, we are sure, are timeless: not historical but human.

Predictably, therefore, critics concerned to assemble the evidence of Hawthorne's anticipations of modern psychology have worked with an agreeable sense of their own inevitability; and, happily persuaded of the primacy of their project, they have tended to mock the interest of history as merely academic.[6] Argued out in full, however, their case might demand great philosophical acumen indeed. How did we become *so* sure of the network of propositions that underlies our belief in "the literary" as an infallible index of "the human"? And what are the practical implications of this complex faith? May not imagination look to the condition of an historic community as well as to the structure of the psyche or the state of the soul? Must literature treat even politics as but a department of psychology?

Of course the "historicist" position is not without its own difficulties. If change is so radical a fact of human experience, how can we recover a meaningful sense of the past at all? Perhaps, on this "Heraclitan" view, its patterns of experience were *so* different as to escape present categories altogether. Or, to state the problem from the opposite perspective, surely we would not read *any* text if we expected to encounter an alien mentality, one that utterly eluded the scope of our own concepts. Thus a radical skepticism, very hard to reconcile with the nature of intellectual inquiry as we understand it, may lie in wait for those who would reject "essentialism" altogether. The river of thought in which we step had better be *somewhat* the same. Yet even as we are forced to accept some version of Emerson's dictum that "there is only *one mind*,"[7] we may yet resist the conclusion that psychological theory (or psychoanalytic practice) has yielded up a science of all its various moods and behaviors. And we can maintain, quite apart from questions of structure, that shifts of attention and varieties of expression are significant enough to arouse and satisfy a curiosity about human difference over time, that the writings we preserve as literature are competent to inscribe difference as well as sameness, that these two may be about equal as possible reasons to read literature.

And, finally, since readers always will, we may as well premise that they may, judge for themselves: can a modest familiarity with the issues of America's colonial history offer any useful hypotheses for the interpretation of Hawthorne's early tales? If not, why have they made themselves so pedantically correct about such matters? Or if so, how may the construction of this "American Studies Hawthorne" come to modify our sense of "Hawthorne's Psychological Themes"? Perhaps these tales are trying to force us to learn something. And once we recover from the shock to our literary sensibility, we might come to like that fact.

40

2

One is always tempted to begin with a "Puritan" tale – the sort we associate with the "solitary" Hawthorne who, just after college, spent twelve or so years living in the home of his mother's family, reading his way through the Salem subscription library and trying (unsuccessfully) to put together several collections of tales of his "Native Land" which, however "Provincial," must yet have its own "Story."[8] From among that group, it is almost irresistibly tempting to select the widely discussed "Young Goodman Brown," which clearly invokes the (mis-)deeds of some of Hawthorne's Puritan ancestors, but also suggests other, more "profound" considerations. Yet even this prime exemplum may need to be placed within the range of Hawthorne's interest as a writer of historical fiction.

Published in 1835, after the breakup of the collection for which it was intended – and which may well have provided it with an important narrative setting – it is by no means Hawthorne's first meditation on the question of New England "witchcraft." Earlier treatments date back to his first projected collection (of 1827 or earlier) and reveal a more Gothic literary style. Clearly Hawthorne's concern was a developing one. Nor does it in any way epitomize his interest in "The Matter of Puritanism."[9] The dark mood which concludes the fictional life of Goodman Brown has often suggested some psychic kinship with the somber and solitary experience of Parson Hooper in "The Minister's Black Veil" (1836); but as Hooper's revival of Puritan gloom seems much more deliberately self-cultivated, his tale may involve other issues altogether; particularly when we learn to date its action well into the eighteenth century.[10] And elsewhere the terms are noticeably different. "The Gentle Boy" (1832) tells a sad enough story – of family disruption in the midst of sectarian dispute – but it dwells at some length on the domestic issues so popular in the fiction of the period. And a fair number of Hawthorne's Puritan tales seem not moodily spiritual at all but quite frankly *political.*

"The Gray Champion" (1835) and "Endicott and the Red Cross" (1838) both profess to find predictions of the American Revolution in acts of resistance of the most local and Puritanic sort; and even

"The May-Pole of Merry Mount" (1836), often treated as a moral allegory, may fit this typological model as well as any other. When John Endicott cuts down "the only maypole in New England" (368),[11] his action may seem less political than when he rends "the Red Cross completely out of the banner" (548) of the realm of England; but only until one learns the current status of this immemorial or mythic symbol. Legitimized – even recommended – by the King himself, maypole ceremonies had become, by the late 1620s, an important symbol by which England's civil religion distinguished itself from its Puritan antagonist.[12] In both cases, therefore, Endicott implies the disestablishment of an "Anglican" religion in the transatlantic territories of *New* England. And most fully evincing this care for ancestral politics, the four tales of the Revolution known as "Legends of the Province House" (1838) discover the legacy of Puritanism at work not in experiences of dark moral privacy but in a rhetoric of resistance and destiny.

The distinguishing mark of "My Kinsman, Major Molineux" (1832), in this context, is that it is frankly political without being very noticeably "Puritan." Few readers can resist its implication of interest in the American Revolution, but its point of literal reference is in fact the 1730s. And its way of being "proleptic" is not quite like that of "The Gray Champion" or "Endicott": what it offers is not some mysterious prefiguration, in a minor historical event, of a major religious apocalypse, but only the more ragged sense that what happens in a well forgotten episode of mob violence is not *so* different from the Event which everyone has agreed to remember. Evidently Hawthorne's interest in "The Matter of the Revolution" was not limited to the terms of Puritan typology. What this suggests, further, is that Hawthorne's reading in colonial history may have been more purposive than is sometimes assumed.[13]

Especially instructive, in this regard, are the terms of the unresolved critical debate on the "Molineux" problem. A rare case in the annals of Hawthorne criticism, the tale was given its first professional sponsorship by "historicists," powerfully persuaded that Hawthorne's account of the violent expulsion of a Tory leader was meant to prefigure the loss and gain – or the imputed guilt – of America's separation from England. Psychoanalytic readers protested, almost at once, that the true interest in the story is the *personal* one, of Robin's ambivalent search for some indulgent paternal influence, and that the "revolutionary" violence which engulfs him is itself best understood as a resistance to "the father"; thus all historical readings unduly particularize the tale. Yet the discovery of names and faces and issues sharply relevant to America's provincial circumstances has caused the particularist reading to remain strong, encouraging a sort of polite compromise: In this story, perhaps, political revolution and oedipal overthrow simply figure one another, endlessly, without subordination or primacy of interest.[14]

On this supple premise, the American Revolution comes to seem just like the act or process of growing up – painful and even violent, as the overthrow of paternal authority must always be, whether literal or figurative; yet not less inevitable for that reason, as nations, just like young men, must surely assume their own "separate and equal station." Still, the scrupulous reader may observe that this conciliatory view quietly elides the one consideration the tale tries hardest to problematize: the intriguing but not always attractive question of "conspiracy."

Quite obviously, most of the story's broad humor and all its irony about "shrewdness" depend on the fact that Robin is the only character in the story who does not know what the local politicos have in store for his kinsman, that very evening. Robin has stumbled into something, well over his head, and its planned events take place in total disregard for his own psychic case. He is forced to grow up, we might say, *just when* some other men are plotting the ouster of an obnoxious local authority, but the logic of the two events is separate enough. It may flatter some theorists to observe that he does, momentarily at least, join in with the general will to revolt. But plots and cabals are entirely alien to his countrified adolescence. And – as it would be naive to suppose that a tar-and-feather procession has come about in a purely natural "course of human events" – we are left with an important reminder: Revolutions are plotted in a way that maturation never is. To imply that the one is as natural and inevitable as the other is to obscure the question of political responsibility.[15]

Some of the tale's best ironies touch just this question of con-

43

spiratorial difference. At a moment of potential clarification, Robin asks the stranger who joins him at the meetinghouse if he " 'happen[s] to know' " the fellow with the face painted half-red and half-black. " 'Not intimately,' " comes the reply, " 'but I chanced to meet him a little time previous . . . [and] you may trust his word . . . that the Major will very shortly pass through this street' " (82). Obviously the stranger *knows*. And surely his answer is as ironical as Robin's question is innocent: Needing to be in just the right place at just the right time, he has met with the man (of a lower social order) delegated to head the parade which he and other, more powerful but less conspicuous leaders have carefully arranged. Evidently nothing like "chance" was in any way involved. Clearly it is only Robin himself who just happens to be there, where the Molineux procession is duly scheduled to pass in review.

Not coincidentally, perhaps, the same sort of irony is playing about the tale's curious headnote. After rehearsing some arcane materials from the "annals of Massachusetts," an obviously learned narrator seems suddenly anxious to spare us a "long and dry detail of colonial affairs"; but when his forgiving formula suggests that "the following adventures . . . *chanced* upon a summer night, not far from a hundred years ago" (68, my italics), we recognize a first version of the forget-real-politics fallacy the tale itself exists to identify and undo. For only in pure romance would all this ritual activity just "happen" to provide the context for an aspiring hero's *rite de passage*. The American Revolution was nothing such. And not even Shakespeare's "Dream" reads this way any more.

Most readers can appreciate the pace and the pathos of Robin's "evening of ambiguity and weariness" (80) without knowing the cause and extent of the rum riots of the 1730s. They may even get along without recalling that a certain kind of nepotistic politics had once acquired the name of a "Robinocracy." But the story of American political resistance in the eighteenth century is no longer credible without reference to the mob actions that were thoroughly stage-managed by the respectable leaders of colonial society.[16] And what is most noteworthy about Robin's psychic adventure is that absolutely nothing in his growing resistance to figures of paternal authority has quite prepared him for this encounter with the pol-

44

itics of "controlled" and "ritual" violence. Adrift in the city, balked at every turn, cudgel in hand, ready to club anyone you please, Robin may seem ripe for a wider rebellion. But his enduring naivete – a type of our own apolitical criticism, perhaps – has no way of coping with the art of overthrow; evidently some other, more circumstantial initiation is yet to be faced.[17]

Yet the logic of "Roger Malvin's Burial" may offer an even more severe education in the competing claims of general principle and historical circumstance. It is, on one hand, the tale most boldly claimed by the psychoanalytic science of Frederick Crews; and indeed the experience of its protagonist seems compulsed and nightmarish even after Crews has recanted his systematic Freudianism.[18] On the other hand, however, it attaches itself to an event far more obscure than the American Revolution or even the Salem Witchcraft. For – apart from the tale's own headnote – what modern reader has even *heard* of "Lovell's Fight"?

Innocent of all such concerns, Crews opposed instead certain orthodox approaches to the case of Reuben Bourne: Unless one were extremely wary about the ending of this disturbing tale, one had better not venture a religious interpretation at all. What happens there is more barbarous than pious or at any rate, more psychologically elemental than rationally moral. Reuben Bourne may feel that "his sin was expiated" (107) in the killing of his son, but (unless one posits a "teleological suspension of the ethical")[19] the issue is not salvation but psychic survival. The plot of which is clear enough: Ineffectually remorseful ever since his abandonment of his prospective father-in-law, Reuben has thwarted himself in business, poisoned his social relations, then wandered compulsively back to the spot where it all began, to expiate in slaughter what began in grief. Obscurely guilty of the death of a figurative father, he frees his tormented soul by killing – not *quite* accidentally – his literal son. "Regeneration Through Violence"[20] with a vengeance.

Chastened, the moralist may protest that it requires less than oedipal theory to notice that Reuben will suffer great distress at the decision he seems forced to make: Heroically, he would like to remain beside his dying companion in arms; as a Christian,

45

perhaps, he would like to "lay down his life for his friend"; yet he is utilitarian enough to realize the greatest good of the greatest number; and he *would* like to save his own skin. He sees at once the truth of Malvin's prediction: Dorcas will be upset at first, but she will come around; things will be awkward in the meantime, but they must be endured. Yet it is this very meantime that Reuben fears he cannot endure: He knows that Dorcas's eyes, if not her voice, will accuse him of cowardice; and he cannot face this re-fracted version of himself. This is why he allows a tough and ruefully smiling Malvin to persuade him that his real project is to go off and seek a means of rescue. Only thus can he save his life and still maintain the standard of heroism objectified in the glance of Dorcas.

Clearly, this old-fashioned psychology is as relevant as Freud. Source critics might even observe that Reuben's moral dilemma is constructed as a traditional "case of conscience," the very sort of problem treated in one of Hawthorne's favorite seventeenth-century authors.[21] Indeed this older style of motive analysis – press-ing rational analysis to the point of disappearance – may even explain why Reuben feels guilty in the first place: not for refusing "the gratuitous sacrifice of his own life," but for "concealment" (98), of both fact and motive, from all concerned. Including himself.

What draws Reuben back, compulsively, to the spot where he left Malvin is the memory of his unredeemed vow. Baffled by his options, Reuben had promised to return, if not to rescue Malvin, then at least to bury him. Yet this becomes impossible the moment he is less than honest with Dorcas: She inquires for her father and, as he rambles on about the terrible complexity of his forest scene, she falsely infers that her father died with Reuben nearby and was buried by him. Reuben merely holds back the truth; yet when she spreads the tale of his wonderful "courage and fidelity" (97), he is trapped in his own deceptive silence. Nor is this "mental res-ervation" unrelated to his original mixture of motive. The situation turns out exactly as he had imagined: She expects heroism and he cannot bear to confess ordinariness; he lets her conclude exactly what he, looking at himself through her eyes, had himself wished to believe. And the whole problem had arisen, some old-time casuist might observe, because Reuben has failed to be clear about his real intentions, to "settle his own motives."

Yet the possible application of moral categories is not at all the main problem with the psychological approach to this tale. The more crucial question, surely, is where either of these analyses leaves the reader who happens to wonder what any of this could have to do with an incident of "Indian warfare" (88). Generalists may prefer to see the tale's headnote as written under a kind of polite erasure. Yet one could also read it as a picque to historical curiosity; and surely no one can *forbid* an inquiry into the possible relevance of "Lovell's Fight."

Source hunters long ago traced a number of the story's symbolic details – Reuben's bloody handkerchief, most famously – to various accounts of what transpired when Lovewell's raiders went out to meet the Natives on a mission of protective retaliation. More recently, a truly inspired sleuth finally discovered the obvious: The oak tree to which Reuben ties that handkerchief looks exactly like the Charter Oak from the flag of Connecticut, held sacred by colonials ever since they hid, in the original, the land titles they meant to protect from the King of England.[22] Evidently the question of bloody wars for territory is supposed to occur to somebody, not utterly distracted by the strife or the delicacy of Reuben's after-the-fact dilemma. For it is after one of the most curious facts in the entire provincial period of New England.

We can – if we think about "The Matter of the Indians" at all – easily imagine that "Lovell's Fight" was probably not a very grand affair, whatever "its consequences to the country"; no doubt its historian can achieve "romance" only by "casting certain circumstances judiciously into the shade" (88). Indeed, Lovewell's men were bounty hunters, seeking Indians at the astonishing value of one hundred pounds per scalp; among other ventures, none very glorious to either side, they managed to kill a small party of Indians while they slept, then got themselves ambushed in pursuit of a single Indian who appeared unarmed but who may have been a decoy. Many of their number were killed outright; some stragglers died in the attempt to return to the settlements; a few escaped to tell the tale.[23] By which tale hangs Hawthorne's own, though this plot might require a little cynicism to predict.

Evidently the first returning witness misrepresented certain circumstances of the expedition – not to his fiancee (though in fact he had been scalping Indians for money to get married), but to his minister who, not unlike the Dorcas of our tale, immediately turned the affair into a ballad of chivalry. His story took hold and was widely republished and rewritten, even after many in Lovewell's town had come to know the less heroic version. With the result that, a hundred years later, just as Hawthorne was graduating from college and preparing to enter the solemn career of making an original American literature out of authentic American materials, a whole culture was preparing to celebrate the centenary of that famous "Fight." One of Hawthorne's professors produced a hymn for the occasion; so did his classmate Longfellow. A Salem newspaper even ran a front-page story on just how and when to hold the celebration.[24] Historical science having recovered the exact date, a pious and grateful people might recall the deeds by which their ancestors had secured the land they now occupied. And – in the midst of a national policy of "Indian Removal" – they would renew their "covenantal" dedication to the same historic values.

The ironies are mostly self-evident. One need not romanticize the Indians to notice that a local embarrassment had been turned into a National Cultural Treasure. People made pilgrimages to a monument erected near "Lovewell's Pond." For the moment, at least, "Lovewell's Rock" was better known than the one filiopietism had tried to drag from the seacoast to the center of Plymouth. And both these monuments – with many others, in fact and literature – expressed the same sense as the famous one at Bunker Hill, the elective destiny of America. Given these circumstances, might one not expect a writer who once suggested building a monument to the supposed witches on the Gallows Hill of Salem Village[25] to mark the occasion in some unorthodox way? And how better than with the story of a would-be hero who spoils life and prevents posterity with an historical lie about the ragged facts of the sad provincial case? For Reuben indeed operates as an historian; and Dorcas too, after she has functioned first as his imagined and then his literal audience. Together they fashion a tale in which, though there is undeniable tragedy, yet everyone acts as nobly as possible and all things turn out for the best. And yet there is, well advertised in the headnote to their fateful little romance, the memory of "certain circumstances" which the interest of history had better not repress. True, it requires a certain determined provincialism to read the tale this way; but the alternative may be just as unsettling. For it may be a good deal easier to rehearse the structure of the psyche than to recover the unlovely actualities of the colonial past. And, as we have yet to suggest, even Hawthorne's Puritan tales may look to circumstances as much as to the soul.

3

The outline of "Young Goodman Brown" is quite simple; but the account it provides seems almost too compressed. A noticeably unsuspecting young man spends a single night in a suspicious-looking forest and returns to spend the rest of an unhappy life suspecting everyone. At one moment this still-resisting protagonist is loudly proclaiming that he "will yet stand firm" (282); but then, in the fluttering of a few pink ribbons, his "Faith is gone." By which he means, shockingly, that "There is no good on earth; and sin is but a name" (283). He may as well give *himself* over to the Devil. It all happens so fast: we seem to have missed something. What power in the world could have utterly overset the painful teaching and sober practice of a whole pious lifetime – transforming a moment of moral panic into a studied and lethal blasphemy? And with such violence?

The narrator suggests, as Brown goes tearing into "the heart of the dark wilderness," that he is simply following "the instinct that guides mortal man to evil" (283). Yet this "Calvinistic" law can account for the direction but not the pace or the timing of Brown's sudden moral collapse: Why had he not been following that path all along? Nor can it quite explain the overdetermination of his new-found despair: Is nihilism the proper opposite of "faith"? Nor does it at all predict the fact that Brown will try to pull himself back from the precipice toward which he is rushing: is it an *evil* instinct which prompts him to cry out to Faith, at the lurid climax of the witch meeting, "Look up to Heaven, and resist the Wicked

49

One!" (288)? Evidently something more is at stake than Melville's suspicion of "innate depravity and original sin."[26]

Something altogether more primal, the psychoanalytic reader is sure to suggest: Brown's readiness to overthrow all authority is instantaneous because it is a given of adolescent experience. And if Brown is a little old for this onset of oedipal hostility, that fact may well account for the rage in his response. His "manhood" has been pent up and smoldering too long; not wisely socialized but too well inhibited by fathers and ministers and even a prim little wife, it will not go forever without finding its moment of eruption. The story merely gives us that moment. As Brown's Devil is nothing more than the emergence of his most unpuritanical unconscious, so the witch meeting in the forest is pure fantasy – for Brown as surely as for his creator. It is not insistently sexual for nothing. And no one should be surprised if Hawthorne chooses the moralistic world of latter-day Puritanism to stand for the problem Freud called "Civilization and its Discontents."[27]

"Be it so, if you will" (288), as the narrator says in response to his own proposed reduction of Brown's twilight-zone experience: There is no reason to suppose Hawthorne believed in the Devil any more literally than do we ourselves; nor need we resist according him a certain prescience about the silent power of sexuality in controlling our motives and centering our identity. Yet Hawthorne's Puritan sources were very much concerned with the question of diabolical agency, and perhaps this provides some other clue to the violence and speed of Brown's rebellious outburst.

It may be only a rare historical joke that the tale evokes Brown's visit to the forest in one of Puritanism's most famous self-descriptions – an "errand" (276) into the "wilderness" (283),[28] but elsewhere the language is as apt as it is official. What it insists is that, however we describe the Devil that erupts from Goodman Brown at the moment of his "horrid blasphemy" (284), another Devil has been conjured well in advance; and that, for all our sense that Brown gets more than he has bargained for, there has indeed been a bargain. From which Goodman Brown tries, at first, to back out: " 'Friend, . . . having kept covenant by meeting thee here, it is my purpose now to return whence I came' " (278).

Brown could hardly have used a more telling and technical word to describe his agreement with the figure who leads him along the forest path. In his world, "covenant" named not only the pact the Calvinist God had made with Christ, by which his obedient sacrifice came to count as reparation for the sins of mankind, but also the agreement by which the saints accepted this vicarious atonement. It served, further, as a mystic substitute for terms like contract or compact in the Puritan's consensual theory of government. And most pointedly, it named the origin and essence of the particular church or congregation. Other churches might claim to exist on some a priori or "catholic" basis, but Puritan churches came into being only when self-professing saints enacted a covenant, among themselves and with God, to walk in His ways. Thus, as historians of witchcraft have pointed out, it could serve to name that unspeakable agreement by which reprobates might swear to walk, antithetically, in the ways of His Archenemy.[29] Well may Goodman Brown hope *this* covenant is not yet sealed.

The fact that Brown manages to avoid parodic baptism *in nomine diaboli* suggests that it is not. And indeed the initial intention of his "errand" seems more tentative than simply to "go over." In the more easily supposable case, someone still failing, after a long and anxious time, to discover any trustworthy signs of election by God might grow desperate; in this mood he might get word that, though God's was surely the only covenant *in town,* there was another, inverted one, off in the forest. The reader of *The Scarlet Letter* will recall that Mistress Hibbins appeals to a despairing Hester Prynne in just such terms; and though Hester resists, the appeal might be very strong indeed. Orthodoxy stoutly held that whole lives might have to be lived out with no assurance beyond that of hope itself, but imagination inferred that here and there some "Ishmael" might despair of ever being recognized as one of God's adopted – declaring, in the formula Emerson made bold to appropriate, "If I am the Devil's child, I will live then from the Devil"; and most suitably, perhaps, if that tortured "I" could share the misery Dickinson called that "white sustenance, despair." A terrible prospect, yet perhaps "a guilty identity . . . was better than none."[30]

But the story of Goodman Brown is a turn more subtle. Setting out for the forest, Brown feels guilty enough about his purposes, yet feels confident that he can make his little visit with impunity: After this one short venture into the Devil's territory, he can safely come back to town, to Faith, to everything as it was. His experiment appears to prove this impossible, but it also suggests, to him at least, that his sense of salvation may have been an illusion all along. And it is this "discovery" which turns his curiosity about the Invisible World into an express confession of diabolical loyalty. Which he then tries to take back.

Brown's wife – Faith, "aptly named," but not yet an allegory we can quite construe – entreats him to "tarry" with her on this "of all nights in the year"; perhaps it is October 31, when evil influences were known to be abroad. But he converts concern into suspicion: " 'dost thou doubt me already, and we but three months married!' " And this curious mood of moral dis-ease continues. His heart smites him, understandably, for leaving his wife "on such an errand!" He even wonders whether "a dream had warned her what work is to be done to-night." But as there is no evidence of this, we infer that Brown's guilt is nervously imagining things. Then, the moment after this recognizable attack of guilty projection,[31] Brown goes on to settle his conscience and compose our allegory: "Well, she's a blessed angel on earth; and after this one night, I'll cling to her skirts and follow her to heaven" (276).

There is a question of gender here, of course, as Brown imagines his wife as a different sort of moral being. But – as it is "with this excellent resolve for the future [that] Goodman Brown felt himself justified in making more haste on his present evil purpose" (276) – there is also the problem theologians have called "presumption," the act of declaring one's salvation already certain, whatever might occur in the rest of one's mortal life. Earlier theorists called it an "unpardonable sin," not because it was the most heinous act or thought they could imagine, but because it made nonsense out of their notion of life, all of it, as a period of testing, during which one might, at any moment, turn one's mind toward or away from the will of God.[32] And not surprisingly, Calvinist thinkers kept having to explain that their idea of eternal predestination, based not on merit, but bestowed as the gift of faith, was not just the latest invitation to this familiar moral evasion. Feeling "justified" – the technical word for one's gratuitous acceptance by God – was scarcely an excuse for laxity or experimentation. For one thing, individual assurance could never be perfect; and for another, it needed to be read from the quality of one's ethical dispositions.[33]

Certainly, therefore, the Calvinists did not intend a moral holiday. Yet they may have opened a crack in the wall of perfect behavior. And Goodman Brown appears to be creeping out at that crack, suspending the ordinary rules for a brief period, but trusting in his safety after all; assuming salvation, it appears, in spite of his devilish transgression. "Presuming on Faith," the conscience of official Puritanism might angrily declare; and invalidating the mystical "Marriage" into the bargain. "I told you so," the older system might smugly observe, and deepen its sense of triumph when Goodman Brown goes on to "despair," the only *other* unpardonable sin; the other way, that is, of nullifying the moral life at a stroke.

Yet Brown's despair is scarcely the normative case. Typically, an individual became aware of sins too great to be forgiven by God himself; this looked like an extreme of humility, but was really a bizarre form of pride, as its anatomists never tired of pointing out. Or else, as we have suggested, a Puritan might simply crack under the strain and accept the worst-case scenario. But Brown's problem is not at all a matter of such gloomy introspection; rather, with the help of his Devil, he comes to suspect the settled appearance of virtue in all his most familiar acquaintances. Then, undone by this challenge to the assumptions of his whole life, he despairs of the possibility of goodness in the world. And so fast that his logic – and our explanation – must be embedded in the terms of Puritan history.

Most simply, perhaps, in the doctrine of "visible sanctity." No fool and no mad zealot, the Puritan knew there were "hypocrites" in the churches of New England. These churches had as their explicit aim to be the purest the world had seen since the Savior had elected His own handpicked disciples. Even He had got one "Judas," and so even the most careful of men in these latter days could hardly fail to make mistakes. But members of Puritan churches who were not Saints – who dissembled or who were simply mistaken about their call from God – were to be the exception. Formally so, since by rule one had to give a public account of this call in order to be taken into "communing" membership. Elsewhere, churches might exist to *produce* saints, little by little; but in the New World Order, churches existed to identify, with all human precision, those whom God *called* to be saints, and to bring them together, visibly, into an exemplary order of holy community.[34]

Trained by their system to recognize one another, the Saints came to rely on one another for support of all kinds. Particularly, perhaps, for mutual sanction: One could *hardly* be sure of one's own election, all by oneself, particularly when the evidences of faith were so much more subtle than the older standard of behavior; then too, if one thought about it, there was the whole Anglo-Catholic world one had left behind, scorning the Calvinist theology of total depravity and irresistible grace as an insult to moral sense, and spurning as utopian the doctrine of visible sanctity. But if the whole group held together in these beliefs, the faith of all might stand. Forswearing the intermediation of priest and sacrament, the Puritan might yet find himself comparing notes: our *nature* is evil, as witness our former lives, but has not God's *grace* introduced a principle of goodness? Truly so? In my *own* case? Well, other people might recognize the grace shining forth from one's halting profession more surely than oneself; and *their* conviction — necessary to admit the would-be saint to the bosom of Faith in any event — might become the surest basis of one's own.

What this interdependency implies is the irreducibly social dimension of Puritan faith, even in so private a fact as one's election.[35] For what if an unhappy Puritan found occasion to doubt the good faith of those very individuals whose assurance of salvation had become so entwined with his own? Honestly explored, these doubts might go straight to the source of his own assurance. Even less radically applied, however, they would amount to a suspicion that the covenanting procedures of the particular church had been an empty formality, unable to discover any appreciable difference between the persons one "had met at the communion table" and those seen "rioting at the tavern" (283). Would this experience not threaten all one believed? Might it not bring on, with only some hyperbole, the nihilistic rejection of everything?

So it turns out for Goodman Brown. And so his particular Devil seems to have foreknown, as the climax of his commencement address only confirms the sense of Brown's mid-forest outburst: Evil is indeed " 'the nature of mankind,' " as Calvin's theory of depravity has prepared you to discover; and now, as there *is* no such thing as regenerating grace, " 'Evil must be your only happiness.' " But the Devil's word to the initiates has another note as well. His welcome to the Community of Evil is, before all else, a farewell to the covenantal delusion: " 'Depending on one another's hearts, ye had hoped, that virtue were not all a dream. Now are ye undeceived!' " (287). And – among all the losses of faith that are possible – this "congregational" circumstance contributes powerfully to making Brown's loss a particularly memorable instance.

Equally important, however, is the logic which effects that undeception. We follow well enough the steps by which Brown comes to feel that he and Faith are "the only pair . . . yet hesitating on the verge of wickedness" (287). If all these trusted and familiar Saints turn out to be the Devil's own, then so must the rest of this wretched world as well. But what *of* those supposed Saints? Has Goodman Brown been reliably informed about their true allegiance? Are they indeed all in league with the Prince of Darkness? Or is there reason to suppose that Brown has been deceived? Could there be something wrong with his evidence, even where plain sight has supplied an ocular proof?

We might begin by recalling that not all that evidence has been visible. The process begins, in fact, with hearsay, a couple of stories about the misdeeds of Brown's ancestors; and though it moves on from there, to the sight of the irreverent Goody Cloyse and the lascivious church officers, there seems no marked change of mood or conviction. The Devil is prosecuting his proper case, and Brown's responses are perfectly continuous: sad business, but no rule for the likes of a "simple husbandman" (279) like me; and besides, there's always "My Faith." Then come the pink ribbons, and it's all over but the blasphemous shouting. Yet not even these most material objects can quite disturb the reader's sense of a single shape and direction – a single epistemology – of the whole sequence. If there is a climax, it involves the ordering of the persons charged rather than the evidence presented. It is as if the line between imagination and being, perception and conviction, suspicion and proof had entirely disappeared; as if one had merely to lead Brown's attention from one fantastic projection to another.

Certainly this impression will be strongest in the reader who notices that none of the characters Brown meets on the forest path seems to cast a shadow, and that they appear and disappear in the most remarkably convenient manner, as if conjured by the Companion's "snakelike staff" (279). Curiosity about this magical quality ought to be enhanced by the observation that each of these exemplary apparitions is referred to as a "figure" or a "shape," as if to reserve judgment on their proper mode of existence. And it is precisely in this mood that a reader may profit to discover – in a learned article by David Levin – the antique doctrine of "specters," those mysterious simulacra of physical appearance which made it possible for persons to appear in places remote from their locus of true and substantial being. And to learn, too, of the controversy, in Brown's own (third-generation) New England, about the Devil's power to manipulate these spectral appearances.[36]

Most authorities taught that the Devil regularly did assume the shape of his sworn disciples – whenever he went abroad to carry out their guilty wishes. And this understanding made it possible for the witch accusers to maintain their allegations against persons who could otherwise account for their whereabouts: I must have seen their *specters*. The crisis arose when someone thought to ask whether the Devil had the power to assume the shape of a person who had *not* freely chosen his covenant, to cause a Saint to appear in the most compromising of places and postures. The magistrates appointed to conduct the proceedings against the accused witches thought a just God would never permit the exercise of a power so fatal to the cause of human faith. But a panel of experts returned the opinion that the Devil might well enjoy that very power: What else could Scripture mean by declaring that "the Devil has appeared as an Angel of Light"?

The story of the events which followed the proclamation of this unsettling possibility has held a terrible fascination for those who have pursued the historical record – including Arthur Miller, whose dramatic rendition (in *The Crucible*) has caused the metaphor of "witch hunt" to stand for all sorts of accusations which admit no refutation. Here, however, there are no courtroom recriminations; and no hint of that general breakdown of faith Hawthorne elsewhere refers to as a "Universal Madness riot in the Main-street" (1047). Only the possibility that Brown may be witnessing not the real activities of his fellow congregationalists but only the meretricious antics of their spectral shapes. We cannot be sure.[37]

In his running contest with the Devil, Goodman Brown has tried to make it all depend on his "Faith"; and so in the end it does, though in a way his presumptuous confidence had little prepared him to expect. Did Faith indeed "look up to heaven and resist the Wicked One"? Was she in fact even there? Or was it her specter, stolen by the Devil for the express purpose of tempting the faith of Goodman Brown? He never can know. She may well be as innocent as Shakespeare's Desdemona – whose innocence, as a modern reading has observed, can never be known by Othello in the same way that *she herself* knows it.[38] Nor can the story itself inform us without entirely compromising its own epistemology: We never do know the intentions of others, not as they themselves know them. As intentional reality is hidden, so all moral appearances are in an important sense spectral: We observe the shape but do not behold the substance. Best to reserve judgment, therefore, ascribing to others, always, the same degree of good faith we habitually discern in ourselves; best to assume that others' resistance to Evil is about equal to our own.

Doubt, in this sense, becomes the source of, even participates in, the nature of faith: The negative term signifies only our unhappiness about the fact that we cannot know certain things for sure; the positive one, our recognition that we have nevertheless to make up our minds and act. All Goodman Brown can know, in the end, is that, after keeping his initial covenant, he recoiled from the Devil's baptism; he flirted with the power of Evil, so to speak, but did not in the end espouse it. Might he not suppose that the wishes of his wife have been equally hypothetical? Failing this sort of ascriptive trust, his final gloom reveals nothing so plainly as the lasting effect of his initial bad faith: The guilty self-knowledge which caused him to suspect Faith of suspecting him assumes its settled form in doubting the victory of her virtue. The problem has its "psychoanalytic" side, of course, but it requires less than a full course of "analysis." For if Brown's bad faith puts forth, from the beginning, the textbook traits of "guilty projection," the same must be said of Spenser's Red Cross Knight, whose deception by the "dreamy" machinations of Archimago had long since suggested that specter evidence is but a curious name for the shameless tendency to discover in others, as fact, the guilty wish we repress in ourselves.[39] And more important, in any case, may be Hawthorne's historical re-application of this Spenserian principle – to a set of theological circumstances that matter as much as the more political ones in "Molineux" and "Malvin."

Not that Hawthorne has solved the question of "What Happened in Salem." It is worth noting that, where his contemporaries tried to rationalize the problem of witchcraft – by invoking the quasi-medical notion of "hysteria," or by appealing to the pseudo-historical idea of "superstition" – Hawthorne is careful to let this limit phenomenon retain something of its terrible wonder.[40] We learn to suspect that people who discover witches are telling us more about themselves than about the persons they accuse; but "Young Goodman Brown" has nothing to say about what persons did and did not indulge this self-betraying behavior.

What this taut little tale observes, instead, is that the discovery of Saints and the detection of witches were parts of the same problem, that specter evidence was simply the negative test case of visible sanctity. In morally opposite but epistemologically identical instances, certain official persons needed to make reliable judgments about the soul *in extremis*. Beyond actions, which are various; beyond even intentions, which may be fleeting and even whimsical; the Puritan had to identify the deep spiritual orientation of another person. Here is a soul, solemnly requesting admission to the sacrament which sets the seal on the mystery of salvation: Is it sworn to God, finally, beyond all possibility of change or mistake? Or, as the curiously unfolding historical plot suddenly reversed itself, has it perhaps made that other oath? Sooner or later, in the latter, parodic instance if not in the former, normative one, this dedicated group of religionists would surely discover that their most important judgments were all more or less projective.

Needing to know what cannot certainly be known – the true spiritual estate of another person – such judges must put in the place where literal "in-sight" is denied a hypothetical version of their own relevant experience.

In the matter of Puritan church admissions, the official insistence that everyone exercise the "judgment of charity" came close to recognizing the peril: judge the faith of others, always, by the light of one's own best faith. But then, by a reversal of logic and a lapse of sympathy one notes without quite understanding, the witchcraft proceedings of 1692 seemed to invert their own rule: Saints are known by faith but witches by suspicion. Indeed, Brown's swift progress – from believing in those who have believed in him, to doubting all virtue but his own – seems invented to mimic the outline of this definitive Puritan dilemma. And though we can learn to state this problem in some remarkably general ways, the story itself seems remarkably loyal to its very own circumstances. By its logic, the history of the lapsed Faith of Puritanism remains a capital way of learning the benefit of doubt.

NOTES

1 The assumptions I ascribe to "most readers" would find support in at least two important modern schools of critical opinion: in the so-called "New Criticism," which insists that literary meaning is entirely "internal" to the text; and also (more recently) in the variety of "Reader Response" theories, which stress the extent to which literary meaning is a production of the individual reader. For a brief exposition of these positions, see M. H. Abrams, *A Glossary of Literary Terms* (New York: Holt, Rinehart, and Winston, 1985), pp. 223–4, 231–4. For more extensive discussion of the theory of internalism, see Murray Krieger, *The New Apologists for Poetry* (Minneapolis: University of Minnesota Press, 1956); *Theory of Criticism* (Baltimore: Johns Hopkins University Press, 1976); and Vincent B. Leitch, *American Literary Criticism* (New York: Columbia University Press, 1988), pp. 24–59. And for a sample of the theories that empower the reader, see Jane P. Tompkins, ed., *Reader-Response Criticism* (Baltimore: Johns Hopkins University Press, 1980).

2 For professional complaint about the unpreparedness of the American

student, see Allan Bloom, *The Closing of the American Mind* (New York: Simon and Schuster, 1987); and E. D. Hirsch, *Cultural Literacy* (Boston: Houghton Mifflin, 1987).

3 For a brief introduction to the incipient theory and practice of the "New Historicism," see Ross C. Murfin, "What is the New Historicism?" in Murfin, ed., *The Scarlet Letter* (Boston: St. Martin's Press, 1991), pp. 333–44. For fuller treatments, see H. Aram Veeser, ed., *The New Historicism* (New York: Routledge, 1989); and Brook Thomas, *The New Historicism* (Princeton, N.J.: Princeton University Press, 1991).

4 For an epitome of the achievement of Hawthorne "source studies," see Neal Frank Doubleday, *Hawthorne's Early Tales* (Durham, N.C.: Duke University Press, 1972).

5 In context, Hawthorne's remark about "burrowing ... into the depths of our common nature, for the purposes of psychological romance" reads not as a rejection of history but as a defense against "egotism"; see Hawthorne's Preface to *The Snow-Image*, in *Hawthorne: Tales and Sketches* (New York: Library of America, 1982), p. 1154.

6 See, for example, Frederick Crews, *The Sins of the Fathers* (New York: Oxford University Press, 1966), especially chap. 2, "The Sense of the Past," pp. 27–43.

7 For Emerson's most famous defense of the proposition that "There is one mind common to all individual men," see "History," in *The Collected Works of Ralph Waldo Emerson*, vol. 2, Alfred R. Ferguson and Jean Ferguson Carr, eds. (Cambridge: Harvard University Press, 1979), pp. 3–23. This essay compresses the argument of his lecture series on "The Philosophy of History"; see *The Early Lectures of Ralph Waldo Emerson*, vol. 2, Stephen E. Whicher, Robert E. Spiller, and Wallace E. Williams, eds. (Cambridge: Harvard University Press, 1964), pp. 1–188.

8 The story of Hawthorne's early career as a writer of tales involves his serious but failed attempts to publish collections of tales which might answer the widespread complaint that America was not a "storied" nation: "Seven Tales of My Native Land," ca. 1825–27; "Provincial Tales," ca. 1828–29; and "The Story Teller," 1831–34. For discussion, see Nelson F. Adkins, "The Early Projected Works of Nathaniel Hawthorne," *Papers of the Bibliographical Society of America* 39 (1945), 119–55; Nina Baym, *The Shape of Hawthorne's Career* (Ithaca: Cornell University Press, 1976), pp. 15–52; and Michael J. Colacurcio, Introduction to *Nathaniel Hawthorne: Selected Tales and Sketches* (New York: Penguin, 1987), esp. pp. vii–xxv.

9 The other early "witchcraft" tales are "The Hollow of the Three Hills"

(1830), originally intended for "Seven Tales," and "Alice Doane's Appeal" (1835), apparently a reworking of an earlier "Alice Doane," probably intended for that same volume. For "The Matter of Puritanism" as but one subject of importance to the interest of an American literature, see Rufus Choate's 1833 Salem lecture on "The Importance of Illustrating New England History by a Series of Romances Like the Waverley Novels," in *Works* (Boston: Little, Brown, 1862), vol. 1, pp. 319–46. For discussion, see Doubleday, *Early Tales*, pp. 24–6.

10 For the significance of the dating of "The Minister's Black Veil," see Michael J. Colacurcio, *The Province of Piety* (Cambridge: Harvard University Press, 1984), pp. 312–85.

11 All citations of the text of Hawthorne's tales, given in parentheses, are from *Hawthorne: Tales and Sketches* (New York: Library of America, 1982).

12 For the English background of the "The May-Pole of Merry Mount," see Doubleday, *Early Tales*, pp. 97–9; and J. Gary Williams, "History in Hawthorne's 'May-Pole of Merry Mount,' " *Essex Institute Historical Collections* 108 (1972), 3–30.

13 In an 1837 letter to former classmate Longfellow, Hawthorne admits he has "turned over a good many books," but only, he protests, "in so desultory a way that it cannot be called study"; see *Nathaniel Hawthorne: The Letters, 1813–1843*, Thomas Woodson, L. Neal Smith, and Norman Holmes Pearson, eds. (Columbus: The Ohio State University Press, 1984), p. 252. For discussion, see Colacurcio, *Province*, pp. 71–8.

14 For the historicist view of "My Kinsman, Major Molineux" (MKMM), see Q. D. Leavis, "Hawthorne as Poet," *Sewanee Review* 50 (1951), 198–205; and Roy Harvey Pearce, "Hawthorne and the Sense of the Past," *ELH* 21 (1954), 327–34. For the psychological response, see Hyatt H. Waggoner, *Hawthorne* (Cambridge: Harvard University Press, 1955), pp. 46–53; and Seymour Gross, "Hawthorne's MKMM: History as Moral Adventure," *Nineteenth-Century Fiction* 12 (1957), 97–109. For the attempt at reconciliation, see Robert H. Fossum, *Hawthorne's Inviolable Circle* (Deland: FL: Everett/Edwards, 1972), pp. 26–31; and Peter Shaw, "Fathers, Sons, and the Ambiguities of Revolution in MKMM," *New England Quarterly* 49 (1976), 559–76.

15 For Jefferson's attempt to "naturalize" the coming of the American Revolution, see Garry Wills, *Inventing America* (Garden City, NY: Doubleday, 1978), pp. 93–110. For an account of Americans' self-forgiving view of their "Coming of Age," see Michael Kammen, *A Season of Youth* (New York: Knopf, 1978), pp. 186–220.

16 On the question of "Robinocracy," see James Duban, "Robins and Robinarchs in MKMM," *Nineteenth-Century Fiction* 38 (1983), 271–88. For the management of mobs in eighteenth-century America, see Arthur M. Schlesinger, "Political Mobs and the American Revolution," *Massachusetts Historical Society Proceedings* 99 (1955), esp. pp. 244–50; Edmund S. and Helen M. Morgan, *The Stamp Act Crisis* (Chapel Hill: University of North Carolina Press, 1953), pp. 159–68, 231–40; G. B. Warden, *Boston 1689–1776* (Boston: Little Brown, 1970), pp. 92–101; Gary B. Nash, *Urban Crucible* (Cambridge: Harvard University Press, 1979), pp. 292–311; and Peter Shaw, *American Patriots and the Rituals of Revolution* (Cambridge: Harvard University Press, 1981), pp. 5–47. For application of these matters to MKMM, see Shaw, "Hawthorne's Ritual Typology of the American Revolution," *Prospects* 3 (1977), 483–98; and Colacurcio, *Province,* pp. 130–53 (bibliography, pp. 562–71).

17 For readings which resist the conclusion that Robin has learned his needful lessons – "or will have when apprehension becomes knowledge" (Gross, "Moral Adventure," p. 108) – see John P. McWilliams, Jr., *Hawthorne, Melville and the American Character* (Cambridge: Cambridge University Press, 1984), pp. 85–8; Frederick Newberry, *Hawthorne's Divided Loyalties* (Rutherford, NJ: Fairleigh Dickinson University Press, 1987), pp. 62–5. And for an emerging emphasis on Robin's problems of manhood in a new, urban environment, see David Leverenz, *Manhood and the American Renaissance* (Ithaca: Cornell University Press, 1989), pp. 231–9; and T. Walter Herbert, "Doing Cultural Work: MKMM and the Construction of the Self-Made Man," *Studies in the Novel* 23 (1991), 20–7.

18 For Crews's strictly Freudian reading of "Roger Malvin's Burial" (RMB), see "The Logic of Compulsion in RMB," *PMLA* 79 (1964), 457–65; and cp. *Sins,* pp. 80–95. A more distanced attitude toward Freud is expressed, *passim,* in *Out of My System* (New York: Oxford University Press, 1975); and explicitly revisionary remarks on Hawthorne are offered in *Skeptical Engagements* (New York: Oxford University Press, 1986), pp. xiii–xiv.

19 Thus Søren Kierkegaard has described the "existential" demand of Genesis 22, as a transcendent God requires Abraham (consciously) to sacrifice his son Isaac (but intervenes to provide an animal substitute). For readings which take this religious paradigm as seriously as possible, see Ely Stock, "History and Bible in Hawthorne's RMB," *Essex Institute Historical Collections* 100 (1964), 279–96; and Emily Miller Budick, *Fiction and Historical Consciousness* (New Haven: Yale University Press, 1989), pp. 36–54.

20 Richard Slotkin reads the ending of RMB as an explicit critique of frontier mythology; see *Regeneration Through Violence* (Middletown, CT: Wesleyan University Press, 1973), pp. 477–8, 483–4. On the issue of the frontier in RMB, see also Edwin Fussell, *Frontier* (Princeton: Princeton University Press, 1965), pp. 75–7; Ann Ronald, "Roger Malvin's Grandson," *Studies in American Fiction* 12 (1984), 71–7; and James McIntosh, "Nature and Frontier in RMB," *American Literature* 60 (1988), 188–204.

21 The importance to Hawthorne of the seventeenth-century "casuist" Jeremy Taylor was first established by Neal F. Doubleday, "The Theme of Hawthorne's 'Fancy's Show Box,' " *American Literature* 10 (1938), 431–3. For a full account of Taylor's influence on RMB, see Colacurcio, *Province*, pp. 109–14.

22 For the *realpolitik* of Hawthorne's "symbolic" tree, see John Samson, "Hawthorne's Oak Tree," *American Literature* 52 (1980), 457–61. Earlier source studies include G. Harrison Orians, "The Source of Hawthorne's RMB," *American Literature*, 10 (1938) 313–18; David S. Lovejoy, "Lovewell's Fight and Hawthorne's RMB," *New England Quarterly* 27 (1954), 527–30; and Stock, "History and Bible." For full-scale thematic uses of these materials, see Robert J. Daly, "History and Chivalric Myth in RMB," *Essex Institute Historical Collections* 109 (1973), 99–115; and Colacurcio, *Province*, 107–30 (bibliography, pp. 556–62).

23 For the factual account of the Lovewell affair, see Fanny Hardy Eckstorm, "Pigwacket and Parson Symmes," *New England Quarterly* 9 (1936), 378–402; and Gail Bickford, "Lovewell's Fight, 1725–1958," *American Quarterly* 10 (1958), 358–66. But for a reading of RMB which insists we not romanticize the Natives – and which challenges the ironic reading of Hawthorne's headnote – see David Levin, "Modern Misjudgements of Racial Imperialism in Hawthorne and Parkman," *Yearbook of English Studies* 13 (1983), 145–58.

24 *Salem Gazette* (15 April 1825), p. 30; for analysis, see Colacurcio, *Province*, pp. 128–30.

25 Near the end of "Alice Doane's Appeal," the narrator suggests that as we "build the memorial column on the height which our fathers made sacred with their blood," so "here" – on the Gallows Hill – "should arise another monument, sadly commemorative of the errors of an earlier race, and not to be cast down, while the human heart has one infirmity which may result in crime" (*Tales*, p. 216).

26 For Melville's response to "Young Goodman Brown" (YGB), see "Hawthorne and his Mosses," conveniently reprinted in the Norton

Critical Edition of *Moby-Dick,* Harrison Hayford and Hershel Parker, eds. (New York, 1967), pp. 535–51.

27 For more or less Freudian readings of YGB, see Crews, *Sins,* pp. 98–106; Reginald Cook, "The Forest of Goodman Brown's Night," *New England Quarterly* 43 (1970), 473–81; and Edward Jayne, "Pray Tarry with me Young Goodman Brown," *Literature and Psychology* 29 (1979), 100–13. For a newer style of (Lacanian) analysis, see Elizabeth Wright, "The New Psychoanalysis and Literary Criticism," *Poetics Today* 3 (1982), 89–105.

28 "Errand into the Wilderness" titles an election sermon delivered in Massachusetts in 1670 by Samuel Danforth; in after years, that much referenced sermon lent its title to one of Perry Miller's most probing inquiries into the Puritans' original motive and latter-day morale. For a brief application, see Bill Christopherson, "YGB as Historical Allegory," *Studies in Short Fiction* 23 (1986), 202–4.

29 For the full *valeur* of "covenant" in the Puritan world, see Perry Miller, *The New England Mind: The Seventeenth Century* (Cambridge: Harvard University Press, 1939), 365–462. As Miller notes elsewhere, "the heinousness of [the] crime [of witchcraft] was the fact that it, like regeneration, took the form of a covenant"; see *The New England Mind: From Colony to Province* (Cambridge: Harvard University Press, 1953), p. 193.

30 For the theology of Ishmael (and Isaac), see Thomas Werge, *"Moby-Dick* and the Calvinist Tradition," *Studies in the Novel* 1 (1969), 484–506. The Emerson quotation is from "Self-Reliance," the Dickinson from "I cannot live with you" (640). The verdict about a "guilty identity" is adapted from that of Crews on Hawthorne himself (*Sins,* p. 38).

31 For the psychology of projection in Hawthorne, see Crews, *Sins,* esp. pp. 53–60.

32 For a review of the traditional theology of presumption and despair as applied to YBG, see Joseph T. McCullen, "YGB: Presumption and Despair," *Discourse* 2 (1959), 145–57.

33 The so-called Antinomian Controversy (of 1636–1638) – subtly evoked by Hawthorne's sketch of "Mrs. Hutchinson" (1830) – settled the point that, despite the public objections of Ann Hutchinson and the fine distinctions of John Cotton, "sanctification" (the observable ability to obey divine law) would clearly follow as a proper effect of "justification" (the private revelation of a person's acceptance by God); see Miller, *Seventeenth Century,* pp. 389–92; Edmund S. Morgan, *Puritan Dilemma* (Boston: Little Brown, 1958), pp. 134–54; and Wil-

liam K. B. Stoever, *A Faire and Easie Way to Heaven* (Middletown, CT: Wesleyan University Press, 1978), esp pp. 21–33. For application of these concerns to YGB, see James W. Matthews, "Antinomianism in YGB," *Studies in Short Fiction* 3 (1965), 73–5; Claudia G. Johnson, "YGB and Puritan Justification," *Studies in Short Fiction* 11 (1974), 200–3; and Jane Donahue Eberwein, " 'My Faith is Gone': YGB and Puritan Conversion," *Christianity and Literature* 32 (1982), 23–32.

34 For the uniqueness of the "congregational" polity, see Miller, *Seventeenth Century*, pp. 432–62; and Edmund S. Morgan, *Visible Saints* (Ithaca: Cornell University Press, 1963), pp. 1–112. The remnants of this system lasted well into Hawthorne's own century, but the basis of his scholarly knowledge of the problem may well have been Book 5 ("Acts and Monuments of the Faith and Order in the Churches of New England") of Cotton Mather's *Magnalia Christi Americana* (London, 1702).

35 Though Miller implies that the Puritans' "subjective insight" and "obsession with individuality" (*Seventeenth Century*, p. 22) are balanced by their sense of the particular church as "the center of a communal system" where "the fraternity was made one by their mutual and irrevocable pledge" (p. 443), we still lack a convincing account of the overwhelming commitment to community we sense in the pages of Bradford's *Plymouth Plantation* and Winthrop's "Model of Christian Charity." For the best available study of the social dynamics of the profession of "saving faith" – made for the judgment and edification of the entire congregation – see Patricia Caldwell, *The Puritan Conversion Narrative* (Cambridge: Cambridge University Press, 1983), esp. pp. 45–116.

36 See "Shadows of Doubt: Specter Evidence in Hawthorne's YGB," *American Literature* 34 (1962), 344–52. Levin provides an extremely useful collection of texts and documents related to the "spectral" question of 1692 in *What Happened in Salem* (New York: Harcourt, Brace & World, 1960). For a full-scale account of YGB as a crisis in the Puritan theory of evidence, see Colacurcio, *Province*, pp. 283–313 (bibliography, pp. 610–17). And for an attempt to generalize the notion of spectrality to cover the question of history, see Budick, *Historical Consciousness*, pp. 79–97.

37 This "undecidability" lends some credence to a "postmodern" reading; see, for example, Christopher D. Morris, "Deconstructing YGB," *American Transcendental Quarterly* 2 (1988), 22–33. And yet, as Goodman Brown is forced to make *some* decision, the story appears to concern faith more properly than signifiers. Clearly (in any case) it is

65

shortsighted to claim that the issue of specter evidence causes us to blame the Devil and excuse Goodman Brown; see Paul J. Hurley, "YGB's 'Heart of Darkness,' " *New England Quarterly* 37 (1966), 410–19.

38 See Stanley Cavell, *In Quest of the Ordinary* (Chicago: University of Chicago Press, 1988), p. 55.

39 For Spenser's influence on Hawthorne's theme of specter evidence, see John Schroeder, "Alice Doane's Story: An Essay on Hawthorne and Spenser," *Nathaniel Hawthorne Journal* 4 (1974), 129–34; and Colacurcio, *Province,* pp. 84–5, 295–7.

40 For the inceptive version of the nineteenth-century view of the Salem witchcraft as a combination of outmoded superstition and the deleterious influence of Cotton Mather, see Charles W. Upham, *Lectures on Witchcraft* (Boston, 1831).

World Lit Hawthorne: Or, Re-Allegorizing "Rappaccini's Daughter"

CAROL M. BENSICK

L ITERATURE professionals used to maintain that the characteristic of "great" literature was universality. As a corollary, localism, in space or time, was an artistic fault, at least in literature that wanted to be great. Then, they used to maintain that "Rappaccini's Daughter" was great. This must have meant that teachers and critics did not detect in it any insistence on period or place, or parochial or transitory theme. They must have supposed that it had universal concerns. And they must have been glad that it did.

Times have changed. "Rappaccini's Daughter" – long viewed as being "one of the tales by which we measure the greatness of Hawthorne's tales" is now routinely denigrated. It is accused of "artistic confusion," or it is found positively "contradictory." And a recent, denigrating discussion of the tale finds fault with it precisely on the grounds that "topicality" on the one hand, and "Americanness" on the other – just the kinds of things that for a simpler time would have crippled a work with designs on greatness – are *not* there.[1] But what is lack of topicality but universality in time? And what is lack of Americanness but the same in space?

There is another noteworthy way in which times have changed in "Rappaccini" studies. The tale not only looks worse to contemporary eyes; it seems to have a different subject. It used to be a virtual cliché that "Rappaccini's Daughter" was about religion. Now (after a brief interval when it was about interpretation), it is about women in Hawthorne's life (variously his wife, his newborn daughter, his younger sister, an old girlfriend); or it is about stereotypes of women in popular culture; or it is about Hawthorne's uneasiness about virility; or it is about "intercultural romance."[2]

In all cases, it is again, as it had been when criticism on it began, and after a considerable spell in which it had become about its themes, about its characters. The new readings are not notably less allegorical than the religious ones; the characters still refer but what they refer to are not ideas but individuals or classes of people.

A further peculiarity of the times in "Rappaccini" criticism is a prevailing disposition to ignore what had formerly seemed objective accomplishments in establishing a context for the tale, the illuminations not of dogma or doctrine but of intellectual history. One would think that the identification of the Transcendentalist–Unitarian "Miracles Controversy" in Jacksonian New England, the "Immortality Controversy" among competing schools of Aristotelians and between academics and the church in Renaissance Padua, and perhaps of the controversy over medical empiricism in the latter place would have permanently affected readings of the story.[3] These viewpoints the majority of younger commentators, however, simply ignore.

One recent voice, that of John N. Miller, even makes them the object of ridicule. According to Miller "Rappaccini's Daughter" has divided critics into two camps. (Since his account is not actually chronological, to call these "old" and "new" is a little slippery. Yet this dichotomy, so convenient and so familiar, can be defended on the score of the spirit of the different contributors' projects, if not of their age.) The old school was both "historical and deconstructive." The young critics, in contrast, are committed to "biographical data." The former were interested in "background reading and intellectual *zeitgeist*." The latter are concerned with "the author as a complex historical literary and emotional being." They are the champions of "the tale itself." The former care only for their own "rarified [sic] context." On the one side, we find a defense of "Hawthorne's artistic and intellectual control"; on the other, a sympathizing re-creation of "Hawthorne's own problem." According to which school you adhere to, "Rappaccini's Daughter" is finally a tale to be approached through "theological controversy and intellectual history," or it concerns Hawthorne's "own ambivalence about the women closest to him." In a comprehensive gesture of dismissal also found in the comments of Luther Luedtke and Edwin Miller, John Miller plangently inquires:

"May we not grant the same respect" to "evidence of biographical antecedents for Hawthorne's Beatrice" as the scorned "Hawthorne scholars" have granted to "Dante's Beatrice, Beatrice Cenci, and even God's or Adam's Eve?"[4]

Some suggestions from the discredited "historical and deconstructive" school seem to have been accepted. For example, it is now evidently impossible to refer to the "I" speaker in the text as "Hawthorne" without acknowledging that a succession of critics have insisted on the necessity of a separation. Miller rejects "a distinction," which he assumes to be consensual, "between *author of* and *storyteller* in Hawthorne's tale." Yet his recurring reference to the speaking voice of the tale as "Hawthorne or his narrator" (or "author or narrator") is clearly his concession that "this is a valid distinction." And it is now apparently quite difficult to ignore the time and place of the story's action. I put the period of action at 1527–1533 and Robert Gale, in his new *Hawthorne Encyclopedia*, also places the events of the story in this period. Though it has nothing to do with his argument, Luther Luedtke includes an extended footnote in which he uses evidence that Arabic influence prevailed in Padua beyond this period to acknowledge the justness of these claims.[5] But gestures of critical lip service to the contrary notwithstanding, the "I" is still generally understood as being Hawthorne. Convinced that "Hawthorne is simply voicing his authorial and personal outrage against Giovanni," John Miller "substitut[es] *author* for *storyteller*" in a quoted remark of mine to bring out the secret association between the fictitious character of Beatrice and "Hawthorne's once-idealized bride."[6] Though no one denies that the action occurs in a specific period in Padua, this is not permitted to bear on the tale.

Since I am one of those insisting on both the specificity of period setting and the disparity between author and narrator, I may be expected to grumble. But I feel no such impulse. Rather than blame other readers for failing to embrace my hypothesis, I would continue to ask what light it sheds. Making a point of distinguishing author from narrator was a device to facilitate the attribution of a degree of irony to the implicit author. But the evaluation of present attitudes toward approaches to "Rappaccini's Daughter" through intellectual history seems more urgent. Miller properly identifies the intellectual–historical approach with scholars whose historical interest is largely medical. One of these dismisses my attempt to associate the Baglioni character with a range of Renaissance churchmen and philosophers because these candidates are left "hanging in the air." Though seemingly justified, this charge targets intellectual history in general.[7] To properly assess Miller's charge that the approach from intellectual history is too "rarefied" one should recall how such an approach to Hawthorne arose. It did so through the tracing of sources, sources identified by allusions which were in some cases words, phrases, or images embedded in the text. These slumbered unrecognized until the eye of someone who happened to have read the same work as Hawthorne fell across them. Since Marion Kesselring's publication in 1949 of Hawthorne's library charge records to 1850, scholars have been able to recognize a greater number of these buried allusions. And where they led was not to literary "precursors" such as Spenser, Milton, or Shakespeare but to argumentative predecessors, past or contemporary. For "Rappaccini's Daughter," the prime source of this kind, as Colacurcio has shown, is George Ripley, metaphysician of religion, source of the tale's insistent language of "evidence."[8]

In general, my present (partial) view of the current state of "Rappaccini" commentary comes down to something like the following. I find it wholesome to father the sayings of the tale, with due irony, on Hawthorne. But discarding the distinction between Hawthorne and narrator also permits recognition, that in disagreeing about "the narrator" we are making rival claims about Hawthorne. And as I am now moved to reunite Hawthorne with his narrator, I should like to adopt an approach to the tale's "interpersonal drama" that is allegorical and even thematic. My former account of "Rappaccini's Daughter," through reference to the phenomenon of Renaissance syphilis, called attention to the literal, empirical, detail in the tale, turning attention away from thematic and allegorical readings. As they became entrenched in places like anthology headnotes, approaches through theme and allegory had grown stale. All too often they reduced and oversimplified the action. At present, however, I see what I want to call the "carnal" approach I had advocated now threatening to be used not as a

corrective but as an end in itself. If criticism formerly needed ma-
terializing, it now needs a new idealization. Today, I am even
prepared to contend for the presence of particular allegorical
themes, themes that are radically religious in nature.

This reversal may seem a manifestation of neoorthodox zeal.
The heatedness of contemporary dismissals of religious–allegorical
interpretations of the story suggests that this is one approach that
current views will not tolerate and cannot contain. But, though
somewhat resembling the old spirit of Hyatt Waggoner and Roy
Male, my present position does not come from them. John D.
Haslett has observed, in a recent article (less a contribution to the
"new" "Rappaccini's Daughter" I've been evoking than a survival
of the "deconstructive" school) that any reading that uses history
to de-allegorize Beatrice absolutely forbids itself to share, as mine
tried to do, the fruits of the readings through intellectual history.
Those readings, whether by Colacurcio, Daly, or William Shurr,
all depend on an allegorical Beatrice; my own Renaissance his-
toricization tended to make the tale all vehicle and no tenor.[9] The
ultimate argument for treating Beatrice through allegory, I now
believe, derives from the co-presence in the tale of a character
named Beatrice and an allusion to Dante. Readers will recall that
"Giovanni is not unstudied in the great poem of his country" and
wonders whether his *pensione* is not the former home of "one of
the partakers of the immortal agonies of the Inferno" (976), and
there has been considerable critical comment on the point.[10] Critics
who treat Beatrice allegorically are not injecting anything into the
tale. They are merely obeying its signal. Her character might be
an imitation of Dante or, at the other extreme, a satire of him. At
the very least, to approach Beatrice through Dante – that is, allegorically – entails fewer restrictions on the critic than does the
determination to connect her with a woman out of Hawthorne's
biography.

Miller pursues his attack on intellectual history (which he nick-
names, synecdochically, "fideism," the term used by Daly in that
tradition) in the name of "allegory." What Miller actually means
by allegory, however, is far from what is conventionally understood by that term. Rather than an author's premeditated scheme
of meaning, Miller's allegory is the author's unconscious projection

into his fiction of his own sexual biography. Miller's supposed defense of allegory is actually an attack on it. The story does not refer to the Miracles Controversy, the Immortality Controversy, or the Syphilis Controversy. The story does not name Ripley, or Pomponazzi.[11] To assume Hawthorne's deliberate intention to imply these subjects requires allegory as a premise.

To refuse to concede an abstract, intellectual dimension to the interpersonal drama in "Rappaccini's Daughter," to insist, rather, on a strictly carnal one as Poe did when reading "The Minister's Black Veil" as a mystery hinging on Parson Hooper's sexual sin,[12] seems undesirable in two respects. It flies in the face of the Hawthorne who could wish for the endurance of human history "until some great moral shall have been evolved" (742). But the refusal to treat Beatrice Rappaccini as intelligibly charged with some sort of religious meaning has more definite consequences. De-allegorizing Beatrice in its final effect trivializes a tale for which, many signs suggest, Hawthorne was deliberately ambitious. In a tale dealing, as currently held, with sex (or at least gender) – or fixing, as I had argued, on syphilis – allusions to Cellini and the Borgias may pass for window dressing. An invocation of Dante would be quite unnecessary, not to say pretentious. Other matters turned up by the slightest efforts at research could be accounted for only in the manner of Edwin Miller, as a desperate and futile effort on Hawthorne's part to hide the secret truth about his own dirty mind.

Yet here are a few of such referential items. The Baglioni character's "play's the thing" fable – designed within the fiction to impel Giovanni to convey the experimental potion to Beatrice and functioning for Hawthorne as a means to bring on his intended climax – is a complex allusion to Aristotle. Beatrice's last speech contains a concise refutation of an axiom in Machiavelli's *The Prince*. The wine that Baglioni offers Giovanni was created by Voltaire for *Candide,* which, as little effort uncovers, was the last work Hawthorne's notebook records his having read before composing the tale. The current tendency to treat the tale with tools and expectations developed for and appropriate to the realistic novel begins to appear misguided.[13]

As a critical approach, intellectual history may be too rarefied, but remembering Hawthorne's library records, one would rather err in the direction of attributing too many active allusions to a tale than too few. When one knows that "lacryma" (983) is drunk in a book Hawthorne has just been reading, William Shurr's seizing on a literal translation of the name of this wine as a signal that Hawthorne is presenting the Baglioni character as a figure of Christ appears underironic. As for the other effort besides Shurr's to make something of this detail – indicating at least that the odd word must mean something – to one aware of the precedent in *Candide*, the footnote in current editions of the Norton anthology identifying the drink as "a still Italian wine" provokes a sputter.[14]

In the course of his analysis of "The Minister's Black Veil" as hinging on a sex crime, Poe also characterized the tale as "caviare." Only the shrewdest of readers, Poe complained, could see the real point. The rabble would mistake the explicit moral – "on every visage a black veil" (384) – for the true meaning, which for Poe is that Parson Hooper had had a guilty relationship with the girl who dies. Poe would probably have supposed Beatrice's exclamation to Giovanni, "Oh, was there not, from the first, more poison in thy nature than in mine" (1005) to be a red herring, analogous to Hooper's (just quoted) exclamation to Rev. Clark, leaving the real story to be about rape, incest, or the like. Poe's belief that Hawthorne was prone to write "caviare" was, for once, no idiosyncrasy. That passionate Hawthorne admirer, Herman Melville, complained, in an alimentary metaphor, "He don't patronize the butcher; he needs roast-beef, done rare." Some forty years later, Anthony Trollope rediscovered Poe's piscine image for the works like "Rappaccini's Daughter" written at the Old Manse.[15]

For Poe the caviare reading was the carnal one. If "Rappaccini's Daughter" does call for rarefaction in its interpretation, that is not necessarily something to be celebrated. For Poe and Melville, if not Trollope, it was something to regret, if not deplore. And if "Rappaccini's Daughter" is literary caviare, then it seems hard to avoid the corollary that its criticism may need to be caviare as well. Entirely agreeing, then, with the observation with which I began (it was David Reynolds's) that "Rappaccini's Daughter" lacks topicality and Americanness, I would stand it on its head. Lack of topicality and Americanness are the distinctions of this Hawthorne story. It wasn't easy for Hawthorne to get away from topical subjects. Anyone familiar with his works can judge whether it was easy for him to not write about America. The unprecedented distance in space and time from his own historical coordinates in the setting of "Rappaccini's Daughter" represents a departure. So long as he confined himself to the two hundred years of the British in North America the problems Hawthorne could consider were limited. Puritanism was capacious enough to permit reflection on most subjects but not all. If he were ever to become more than one more topical American author in the swarm he was going to have to take higher ground.

By all the signs, this made him nervous. He apparently quite broke down over a title. In its first appearance, in *The U.S. Magazine and Democratic Review,* the story we know as "Rappaccini's Daughter" was named "Writings of Aubépine" and the printing was pseudonymous. Before the publication of *Twice-Told Tales* in 1837, Hawthorne had published under fictitious names. After that book, however, there was no reason to seek obscurity. In what seems another sign of insecurity, he equipped the tale with a preface (975–6). "The May-pole of Merry Mount" had had a headnote, and the first paragraphs of both "My Kinsman, Major Molineux" and "Roger Malvin's Burial" are virtually detachable. Never before, however, had Hawthorne prefaced a tale with a separate foreword. And this preface not only extends the tale by more than six hundred words, it is frankly defensive. It blames the reader in advance, for example, for being likely to leave M. De l'Aubépine "without an audience." It foresees that readers will fail "to take" it "in precisely the proper point of view"; and it rates them for their preference for "Eugène Sue." It establishes that if the tale should seem to fail, this is solely the reader's own fault. Though all his prefaces are more or less embittered, Hawthorne will not write anything quite so aggressive toward his readership (the bitterness of *The Scarlet Letter* preface is toward his dismissers) until *The Marble Faun*'s threat to kill the next person who asks him if Donatello had Vulcan ears.

The "Rappaccini" preface betrays anxiety about the tale's reception in still other ways. For instance, it includes virtual instructions on how to approach the tale. The putative translator gives the reader a checklist of what to look for: "fancy and originality," "nature," "pathos," "tenderness," and "humor." At the same time, he warns what not to expect: "outward manners" or any effort to make a "counterfeit of real life." More subtly, the reader is adjured not to suppose that the story's conceptions lack "human warmth," or "have little or no reference either to time or space." The reader is directed to look for the center of "interest" among instances of "less obvious peculiarity" in the "subject" than the aforementioned "manners." And not to be distracted by the "imagery" − which, it is hinted, is not so "fantastic" as he may have heard − but to accept the action as having taken place "within the limits of our native earth." If Hawthorne had had confidence that the tale made itself clear, he would surely have resisted the impulse to provide a user's manual.

Beyond its attempts to attract the reader's sympathy by dwelling on Aubépine's little expectation of popularity, and its provision of instructions on how to read the tale, the preface betrays anxiety in yet another major way. What we have described so far has been the business of the first of the preface's two paragraphs. The second paragraph is taken up with a list of previous works by Aubépine. A reminder to the reader that Hawthorne comes before them as the published author of *Twice-Told Tales* seems a guarantee of the new tale's professionalism. Finally, mention of six other post-*Twice-Told Tales* stories conveys the sense that this tale may not be able to stand on its own. In addition, successive printings of "Rappaccini's Daughter" in Hawthorne's lifetime argue for his anxiety about its intelligibility: He revised the text more largely than any other for its book publication. The revisions, moreover, are of a particular tendency. To give one example, Beatrice's claim in the first printing, "The words of Beatrice Rappaccini are true from the heart outward" is changed in the book version to "from the *depths of the heart* outward." This change seems meaningless − artistically counterindicated, even − but it betrays an anxiety to increase definiteness and clarity of message. A variety of evidences, then, indicates that Hawthorne was exceptionally unconfident regarding the finished tale.

If these are signs of nerves, however, they are also signs of something else. They are signs of ambition. There are other such signs. The tale is long. The allusion to Dante provokes comparison with one of the greatest of tale spinners. The story does not, like "The Celestial Railroad," finally permit unconvinced readers to dismiss it as a dream. "The Birth-Mark," the tale probably most similar in situation and theme from the same period of composition, ends with an explicit moral; "The Artist of the Beautiful," one of the titles mentioned in the preface, does so as well. But "Rappaccini's Daughter," uniquely since "An Old Woman's Tale," stops with the ambiguous question of a character. ("Egotism" and "The Christmas Banquet" end with characters' speeches, but they contain the kind of summary of morals voiced by narrators in "The Birth-Mark" and "The Artist of the Beautiful." Since the narrators are highly individualized, there seems little to choose between one procedure and the other.) They are questions that receive no answer: "What do we have here?" (33) and "Is this the upshot of your experiment?" (1005). As a final sign that Hawthorne's intentions for "Rappaccini's Daughter" were distinctly ambitious, no other tale of this second of Hawthorne's major tale-writing periods, and few enough from the previous one, show a comparable lack of humorous relief. (Only "The Gentle Boy" and "Roger Malvin's Burial" come really close.) Even "The Birth-Mark" has its Aminidab. But Dame Lisabetta, his counterpart in "Rappaccini's Daughter," is ultimately as appalling as the rest. "If she was my wife, I'd never part with that birth-mark" (770) clears the air of "The Birth-Mark" considerably. But for any "Rappaccini" character to say, "If she was my girlfriend, I wouldn't care if she were poisonous" is unthinkable.

If Hawthorne consciously took on more in "Rappaccini's Daughter" than he ever had before, he had a powerful incentive. It is scarcely an overstatement to say he had just been challenged. The best critic in the country had, while encouraging him warmly, made strictures which a man "of pride and sensibility," as Hawthorne described himself in "The Custom-House," could hardly fail to resent. That these strictures were printed during a lull in his own production could not have failed to increase their impact. Poe charged him, in two 1842 (belated) reviews of *Twice-Told Tales*, with what amounted to laziness as well as repression. He claimed that most of the ''tales'' were, in fact, essays. He challenged Hawthorne to become more various in the character of his themes, in tone, and even in his subjects. In reference to two tales in particular – ''The White Old Maid'' and ''The Minister's Black Veil'' – he attacked him on the score of ''mysticism,'' a characteristic which, in the case of the latter story, rendered its ''import'' ultimately impossible of penetration. (Poe's analysis of the essential character of Hawthorne's style as ''repose'' must needs be behind the jest in ''The Old Manse'' that Hawthorne and Sophia's visitors there always fell asleep.

I gather support for the hunch that with ''Rappaccini's Daughter'' Hawthorne not only was motivated but positively intended to mount a conscious assault on the Parnassus of major authors from one further order of evidence – his reading. Letters and his notebooks from the months immediately preceding the composition of the story reveal a distinct trend. On the one hand, Hawthorne was teaching himself German by doing a translation of a tale (''The Golden Pot'') by Tieck. This was surely a concession to his new Roxbury and Concord friends, with their Transcendentalist enthusiasm (shared by his wife) for German literature. That many matters in the area of plot, character, and situation in ''Rappaccini's Daughter'' have direct reference to Tieck, has long been suspected and was recently established by Alfred Marks. On the other hand, Hawthorne was simultaneously doing reading of a very different order. His notebook's relegation of *Candide*'s title to a seemingly casual parenthesis, and the further suggestion that its effect on him was soporific, cannot detract from the significance of the fact that after having read Montaigne and, even more recently, Rabelais, *Candide* was the last work Hawthorne read before the composition of ''Rappaccini's Daughter.''[16]

He had borrowed Voltaire – the complete works, in French – from the Salem Athenaeum in the 1820s. Voltaire had already been the object of an allusion – significantly, in his capacity as an historian – in ''Sir William Pepperel'' (173) as well as, I infer, under the name of ''a French philosopher'' lending his pen to Truth in ''The Intelligence Office'' (885). He would yet supply an allusion for Miles Coverdale in *The Blithedale Romance*. Aside from being French (which may have something to do with the preface's presentation of the author as a prolific Frenchman whose works embody "ponderous" "research" into ancient heretical "religion and ritual"), Voltaire, like Hawthorne on his departure from Brook Farm, was an author engaged in producing as much as he could as fast as possible.

The *philosophe* does not appear on the Transcendental reading list as presented in *The Blithedale Romance*. Voltaire is not one of the "foreign standard authors" whose "specimens" we know Ripley translated and to which the "Rappaccini" preface swipingly alludes. In "Earth's Holocaust," composed a little before "Rappaccini's Daughter," a distinct and invidious distinction is drawn between the "small, richly-gilt, French tomes, of the last age, with the hundred volumes of Voltaire among them" and "the current literature [a phrase notably echoed in the "Rappaccini" preface] of the same nation." Voltaire's work "went off" in the bonfire "in a brilliant shower of sparkles, and little jets of flame" but what Ripley translated – Cousin, Constant, Jouffroy, plus probably, Fourier – "burnt red and blue, and threw an infernal light over the visages of the spectators, converting them all to the aspect of particolored fiends." In the same context, Hawthorne cannot resist noting, "A collection of German stories emitted a scent of brimstone" (809). Take that, Tieck. Voltaire had been a hero to Shelley to whom "Rappaccini's Daughter" alludes in more than one way and toward whom Hawthorne's "P's Correspondence" shows Hawthorne was favorably inclined. To Transcendentalist Ripley, however, Voltaire was ammunition for his polemical war with Andrews Norton. Transcendentalist Carlyle was rabidly anti-Voltaire; certain contemporaneous French philosophers, on the other hand, were nostalgic for him as a missed ally in the fight against the pantheism of the Germans.[17]

It is important to pair Hawthorne with Voltaire rather than with Balzac or another novelist, or even with Tieck. The Frenchman is a didactic author, a moralist. Tieck is a fictionist. In the terms Poe had used in his review to distinguish the provinces of the poem and the tale, Voltaire is concerned with Truth, Tieck with Beauty (or effect). The author who prefers the fiction of Voltaire to that of Tieck will never please Poe. The differences between Tieck and Voltaire come to take on the oddest resemblance to what emerges when one juxtaposes two works on similar subjects by Hawthorne and Poe – "Lady Eleonore's Mantle" and "The Masque of the Red Death," let us say.

However anxious he was, Hawthorne seems, in the end, to have been sufficiently satisfied with his experiment in "Rappaccini's Daughter." He reprinted the tale, once without its preface, and he found a title that adhered. Perhaps the strongest evidence that he liked what he had done, however, comes in the piece he wrote to introduce the collection in which it first came before a wide international audience. In *The Old Manse,* he announces a valedictory to "tales and essays." "Unless I could do better, I shall do no more in that vein" (1149). This could be a gesture of self-deprecation. I think, however, it is one of pride. Rather than "these aren't worth doing any more of," his likely meaning is, "I can't do better than these." Even, "Who could?" Not "Eugène Sue," at any rate, to invoke the internationally copied author of *Les Mystères de Paris* mentioned in the preface. Looking at the table of contents of *Mosses,* and asking which one tale likeliest persuaded Hawthorne that he had reached a limit, it is difficult to imagine choosing any but "Rappaccini's Daughter."

NOTES

1 See Michael J. Colacurcio, "A Better Mode of Evidence," *ESQ* 15 (1969): 12–22, esp. p. 20; J. Donald Crowley, *Hawthorne: The Critical Heritage* (New York: Barnes and Noble, 1970), p. 35; John N. Miller, "Fideism vs. Allegory in 'Rappaccini's Daughter,' " *Nineteenth-Century Literature* 46, 1 (Sept. 1991): 223–44, esp. p. 227; and David Reynolds, *Beneath the American Renaissance* (New York: Knopf, 1988), p. 371.

2 Roy Male's *Hawthorne's Tragic Vision* (Austin: University of Texas Press, 1957) is an example of a standard "Christian" interpretation. For a sample reading stressing interpretation, one might see Deborah T. Jones, "Hawthorne's Post-Platonic Paradise," *Journal of Narrative Technique* 18 (198): 153–69. On individual women in Hawthorne's life, virility, and culture, respectively, see J. Miller, "Fideism," pp. 235, 237; Edwin H. Miller, *Salem Is My Dwelling Place* (Iowa City: University of Iowa Press, 1991), p. 252; James R. Mellow, *Nathaniel Hawthorne in His Times* (New York: Viking, 1980), pp. 125–6; David Leverenz,

Manhood and the American Renaissance (Ithaca: Cornell University Press, 1989), esp. pp. 239–44; Luther S. Luedkte, *Nathaniel Hawthorne and the Romance of the Orient* (Indianapolis: Indiana University Press, 1989), p. 181. Because "Rappaccini's Daughter," with "Young Goodman Brown," remains, as Claudia Johnson reiterates, "always . . . the most frequently written about" (*American Literary Scholarship/1986* [Durham: Duke University Press], p. 36) tale, itemizing individual contributions is somewhat distorting. The student's best first move is to consult the relevant chapter, which one wishes could be periodically updated, of Lea Newman's magisterial *Reader's Guide to the Short Stories of Nathaniel Hawthorne* (Boston: Hall, 1979).

3 The Miracles Controversy is history's name for a pamphlet war that occurred in the 1830s between the older and younger generations of Harvard University Unitarian professors and ministers over whether Scripture guaranteed personal immortality historically. The Immortality Controversy is history's name for a sixteenth-century conflict at the University of Padua that occurred between the schools of two rival commentators on Aristotle over whether Aristotle guaranteed personal immortality scientifically. The scholars who argue for the relevance of these two controversies are Colacurcio, "A Better Mode," and Robert Daly, "Fideism and the Allusive Mode," *Nineteenth-Century Fiction* 28 (1973): 25–37. My own argument accepts both these contexts and adds a further layer. I became interested in the sixteenth-century outbreak in the Continental Western European intellectual community of the perennial tensions in medical history between the therapeutic principles of "like cures like" and "contraries cure," between rationalism and empiricism, and between a professional clerisy and lay practitioners. This particular outbreak attended upon the contemporary syphilis epidemic, which followed and was blamed on the return of Columbus's ships from what he thought was India and which produced the collapse of Emperor Charles VIII's siege of the kingdom of Naples due to the illness among his mercenary troops. See my *La Nouvelle Beatrice: Renaissance and Romance in "Rappaccini's Daughter"* (New Brunswick, NJ: Rutgers University Press, 1985). Readers interested in these matters should see, in general, H. G. Koenigsberger et al., *Europe in the Sixteenth Century,* 2d ed. (London: Longman, 1989) and in particular, Claude Quêtel, *The History of Syphilis,* trans. Judith Braddock and Brian Pike (Polity, 1990).

4 J. Miller, "Fideism," pp. 224, 243, 244, 235. The needs of his project require Luther Luedkte to homogenize the practice "in general" of all "critics of the mid-twentieth century." Even more sweepingly, Edwin

Miller makes the "future [i.e., those subsequent to Hawthorne's wife] commentators" on "Rappaccini's Daughter" all one body. In Miller's view, these misguided toilers "have not succeeded in lifting the veils surrounding this tale." Unlike John Miller, Luedkte and Edwin Miller have the excuse for their lack of interest in critical differences that their own projects are only partially critical. See *Nathaniel Hawthorne and the Romance of the Orient*, p. xvii, and *Salem is My Dwelling Place*, p. 252.

5 J. Miller, "Fideism," pp. 234–5, 230, e.g., and *passim*; Luedkte, *Romance*, p. 262; and Robert Gale, *A Hawthorne Encyclopedia* (Greenwood, 1991).

6 J. Miller, "Fideism," p. 235.

7 See Ronald J. Nelson, "A Possible Source for Pietro Baglioni," *Nathaniel Hawthorne Review* 17, 2 (Fall 1991): 17–19, esp. p. 18.

8 See Marion Kesselring, *Hawthorne's Reading* (New York: New York Public Library, 1949), and Colacurcio, "Better." Colacurcio's introduction to *Selected Tales and Sketches [by Hawthorne]* (New York: Penguin, 1987) should also be consulted for an updated version of his argument in short compass.

9 See Hyatt H. Waggoner, *Hawthorne: A Critical Study*, rev. ed. (Cambridge: Harvard University Press, 1963); Male, *Tragic*; Leverenz, *Manhood*, esp. p. 232; John D. Haslett, "Rereading 'Rappaccini's Daughter,'" *ESQ* 35, 1 (1989): 43–68; Colacurcio, "Better," and Daly, "Allusive Mode"; and William Shurr, *Rappaccini's Children* (Lexington: University of Kentucky Press, 1981).

10 Chapter 5 of *La Nouvelle Beatrice* centers on the relevance of Dante with reference to the standard criticism on the topic. A sample essay on the topic written since the book's publication is by Lois Cuddy ("The Purgatorial Gardens of Hawthorne and Dante," *MLS*, 17, 1 [Winter 1987]: 39–53).

11 See J. Miller, "Fideism," pp. 224, 235.

12 Poe's two 1842 *Graham's Magazine* reviews of *Twice-Told Tales* are readily available in anthologies: see, for example, Nina Baym, et al., eds., *The Norton Anthology of American Literature*, 3d ed., Shorter (New York: Norton, 1989), p. 660.

13 Beatrice's dying words are a reversal of a love-versus-fear choice considered in *The Prince*, whereas Baglioni's reference to the family of the Borgia invokes that book's well-known heroes. Aristotle has long been known to Hawthorne scholarship as the "certain sage physician" (996) in the case. Baglioni is suggesting that Giovanni regard him as Aristotle and himself as Alexander. Baglioni's counsel to Giovanni to

imitate Alexander portrays as closely as anything could Machiavelli's wishful advice to Lorenzo dei' Medici to imitate Cesare Borgia. But to cite any of this would be highly misleading. The very point of Hawthorne's history is that it is in the common domain. The exposé model of critical interpretation which is appropriate to and rewarding for Poe (who, we have seen, used it on Hawthorne) is precisely off the point with the New Englander. One cannot too emphatically repeat that the point is not to nail down the *one* model, the *one* source, either with reference to Hawthorne's material or with reference to scholarly finds. The point is that Hawthorne knows everything and knows, moreover, that sooner or later each thing is noticed, and re-noticed, by someone. To try to make a proposition of this: What Hawthorne fiction refers to is History. When it is up to anything, this is what Hawthorne scholarship does too.

14 Shurr, *Rappaccini's Children*, p. 2; and Baym, *The Norton Anthology*, p. 561.

15 See Baym, *Norton*, p. 660; Merrell R. Davis and William Gilman, *The Letters of Herman Melville* (New Haven: Yale University Press, 1960), p 121; and for Trollope, Crowley, *Critical*, p. 519. Melville wrote Evert Duyckinck further that there was "a good deal lacking" to "the plump sphericity of the man."

16 Alfred Marks, "*The Scarlet Letter* and Tieck's " 'The Elves,' " *NHR* 17, 2 (Fall 1991): 1–4; *The American Notebooks* (Columbus: Ohio State University Press, 1972), pp. 241–2, 327, 370, 647.

17 See Perry Miller, *The Transcendentalists* (Cambridge: Harvard University Press, 1950), p. 163; Emile Bréhier, *The History of Philosophy*, trans. Wade Baskin, 7 vols., vol. 6 (Chicago: University of Chicago Press, 1968), p. 107.

4

Ethan Brand's Homecoming

RITA K. GOLLIN

IN THE FALL of 1848, Nathaniel Hawthorne "wrenched" a story out of his "miserable brain" after a long creative drought – "Ethan Brand," about a man who returns home after finding within himself the sin he had long sought, then destroys himself in the kiln where his search had begun.[1] Writing in his native town of Salem, Hawthorne himself had come home after many years, in more senses than one. Like Ethan, he had returned with a mixed sense of inevitability and fulfillment, but he had also returned to his vocation. To resume his old role as writer, he had circled back into his earlier fictions and notebooks to write an almost obsessively controlled story of an obsessed seeker. He patterned the plot, character development, setting, and even incidental episodes as circles within a larger circle defining a return to a point of origin. It is oddly fitting that the story itself circled through several publications before appearing at last in his final collection of short stories, *The Snow-Image and Other Twice-told Tales*.

After returning to Salem in the spring of 1846, Hawthorne felt the peculiarly joyless attachment to his native place that had troubled him since boyhood. In "The Custom-House," he would attribute it to the "sensuous sympathy of dust for dust," and also to the haunting figures of his first Puritan ancestors who had induced in him a "home-feeling with the past." Even while living in Boston and Concord he had "felt it almost as a destiny to make Salem my home," and when he became surveyor of the Custom House, he felt "My doom was on me . . . as if Salem were for me the inevitable centre of the Universe."[2] But the problem went deeper than he admitted, dating at least to his childhood when his widowed mother moved her children into her parental home. There was even then a "coldness of intercourse" between them.[3] As Gloria Erlich puts it, "the split between the ideal mother-centered home of his imagination" and actuality had made " 'home' a problematical matter for him."[4] Like Ethan Brand, Reuben Bourne, and many other characters he had already created or would later invent, Hawthorne now returned to a memory-haunted place that had long been the vortex of his emotional universe. He was happily married, with two children, but with two collections of stories to his credit, he had failed to support his family by writing alone. During the next two and a half years when he managed to fill only a few journal pages, he felt "a gift, a faculty, if it had not departed, was suspended and inanimate within [him]."[5] Finally in the fall of 1848 – possibly spurred by his new role as a manager of the Salem Lyceum, and in that capacity booking such literati as Thoreau and the publisher James T. Fields – his "faculty" revived. While living in a rented house near his childhood home, with his mother and sisters now under his roof, he produced "Ethan Brand," his most intense story about homecoming.

The following spring when Hawthorne was removed from office by the victorious Whigs, he felt "decapitated," as he wryly wrote in "The Custom-House"; pursuing the image with grim satisfaction, he declared he was writing "from beyond the grave." The home town he had returned to was no longer his home. Even his return to it was no longer "a reality of my life."[6] His mother had died, his sisters had dispersed, and he was free to move on.

1

For his setting and most of his characters and episodes, Hawthorne returned to eighty-four pages of notebook entries he had made in the summer of 1838, ten years earlier, during a journey from Salem to the Berkshires and back.[7] A lime kiln on Mount Graylock that he had once inspected by moonlight became the story's focal point. It was a circular stone structure about twenty feet high "with a hillock of earth heaped about the larger part of its circumference" and at the bottom a door "large enough to admit a man in a stooping posture." From the talkative kiln burner on "solitary night-watch," he produced Ethan and his successor Bartram; three

North Adams eccentrics became Ethan's former friends – a stage agent, a one-armed ex-lawyer, and a doctor; a deranged old man became the father of Ethan's victim Esther; a little boy named Joe became Bartram's son; and his vignettes of an itinerant showman and a tail-chasing dog augmented his plot. An 1844 notebook passage supplied the germ of the plot:

> The search of an investigator for the Unpardonable Sin; – he at last finds it in his own heart and practice.

A few lines later, he explored that idea:

> The Unpardonable Sin might consist in a want of love and reverence for the Human Soul; in consequence of which, the investigator pried into its dark depths, not with a hope or purpose of making it better, but, from a cold philosophical curiosity – content that it should be wicked in what ever kind or degree, and only desiring to study it out. Would not this, in other words, be the separation of the intellect from the heart?[8]

That expanded definition adumbrates incremental repetitions in the story Hawthorne wrote four years later. The separation of head from heart, which he had already used for such experimenters as Rappaccini and Aylmer, was now embodied in Ethan Brand.

But Hawthorne imposed a particular kind of circularity on Ethan's story, that of a journey which ends in a homecoming. As Edgar Dryden has observed, Hawthorne's repeated experience "of exile and dispersion from a number of temporary homes . . . is centrally related to his career as a writer."[9] He identified home with the domestic hearth and an integrated self, yet he metaphorically and structurally incorporated in his dramaturgy of homecoming the cycles of dust to dust, sleep to sleep, the day and the year. Through patterns of excursion and return, he expressed anxieties about his habitual solitude, about his vocation, and about mortality itself. Though his metaphors often stretch beyond, the temporary homes in his fiction include the body and the grave.

Home is where the heart is, but the narrators of two early sketches briefly leave home to seek completion. "Homeward! homeward! It is time to hasten home," the narrator declares near the end of "Foot-prints on the Sea-shore" (1838), then repeats, "It is time, it is time." He had left "the haunts of men" to refresh his spirits by wandering along the seashore; but when the sun sinks, "the sea grows melancholy" and the world seems a "desolate waste." Into that desolation, his "spirit wanders forth afar, but finds no resting place, and comes shivering back." Therefore he repeats yet again, "It is time that I were hence," and turns toward home (561, 569).[10] The more complacent narrator of "Night Sketches: Beneath an Umbrella" (1838) ends his outing by resituating the figure of home. After hours of reading, he had gone out in the rain to regain his sense of reality; after "wandering homeless" to the "utmost limits of town," he is ready to head home "straightway." But he pauses to observe a "solitary figure" walking "hitherward with a tin lantern, which throws the circular pattern of its punched holes on the ground around him." Interpreting that multiplied circular image, he says the lantern "will light him back" to the homefire where it was kindled. More platitudinously, he says that if we who are "night-wanderers through a stormy and dismal world . . . bear the lamp of Faith, . . . it will surely lead us home to the Heaven whence its radiance was borrowed" (553–4). Only rarely could Hawthorne himself see by the light of that lamp, as when he assured himself at his mother's deathbed that "God would not have made the close so dark and wretched, if there were nothing beyond."[11]

In "The Old Manse," Hawthorne again ended an account of a brief excursion by fusing secular and religious notions of home, this time in his own voice and without anxiety. As a husband and father, he now had a home of his own, albeit a rented one, and he was out with a friend. After rowing against the current up the Assabeth, "how sweet – as we floated homeward adown the golden river, at sunset – how sweet was it to return within the system of human society." Sweeter still was glimpsing the Old Manse – which had been "a home, for many years" and was "my home, too." Its "homely aspect" now seemed sacred. In that context, he perceived a hound-shaped cloud "couched above the house" as its guardian, and "prayed that the upper influences might long protect the institutions that had grown out of the heart of mankind" (1141–2).

Hawthorne's tightest connection of home and heart is in his happiest homecoming tale, paradoxically the one that most fully anticipates the dark story of "Ethan Brand." "The Threefold Destiny" (1838) also begins when a "world wanderer" returns from a long obsessive quest. Ralph had left to pursue a "high destiny" whose first sign would be a beautiful maiden wearing a heart-shaped jewel, but he now realizes that home is where the heart is. When his old friend Faith says, "You are welcome home," he notices that she is wearing a heart-shaped brooch he had given her "as a parting gift," and accepts the destiny he himself had created. The narrator concludes with an exclamation that "Ethan Brand" undercuts: "Happy they who read the riddle without a weary world-search, or a lifetime spent in vain!" (605–6).

All Hawthorne's fictional homecomings present ironies and riddles that resist solution. Such a riddle is central to "Wakefield" (1837), about a man whose eccentricity derives from – and is defined by – his "uncanny" decision to leave home. When he finally decides to reclaim his hearth and his wife after spending twenty years in the next street, the narrator intrusively warns, "Stay, Wakefield! Would you go to the sole home that is left you? Then step into your grave!" Although the "self-banished man" does not – and cannot – heed him, the narrator berates him as "the Outcast of the Universe" (298). Ethan is even more of an Outcast and knows what his "sole home" is.

The young protagonist of "My Kinsman, Major Molineux" (1832) is also denied a happy homecoming, though chiefly because of his stage in life: He has just left the haven of childhood. Robin comforts himself by thinking of home, drifting into a daydream from which he rudely awakens: "the latch tinkled into its place, and he was excluded from his home" (80). But he has not yet consciously assimilated that exclusion. After he joins the mob in mocking his tarred and feathered kinsman, he wants to turn toward home, but the story ends with a kind gentleman's advice to try rising on his own.

In the more distressing story of "Young Goodman Brown" (1835), the trajectory of leaving home and then returning is completed, unhappily. The man who left Salem expecting to go "forth and back again" before sunset and then cling to his Faith "and follow her to Heaven" returns home as "a stern, a sad, a darkly meditative, a distrustful, if not a desperate man" (276, 288). As

William Blake might put it, the eye altering has altered all. Like Ethan's, Brown's own "evil purpose" has led him astray, and he can have no happy homecoming in this world or (presumably) the next.

In "Fragments from the Journal of a Solitary Man," particularly in the second segment entitled "My Home Return" (1837), homecoming is treated sentimentally. Oberon returns to his birthplace mortally ill, regretting his departure. He had read the rainbow across his path as a sign of good fortune, but he now rereads it as "the ghost of hope" and rhetorically asks, "Why have I never loved my home before?" A mournful embodiment of the young Hawthorne's own worst fears, Oberon had departed "to wander away and return again, with my fate accomplished, and little more hope in this world" (496, 497).[12] Ethan Brand would reach this conclusion more bitterly though more triumphantly.

In "Roger Malvin's Burial" (1832), the associations of homecoming with death are more densely ironic. Years after abandoning the dying Malvin, promising to return to bury him, Reuben Bourne is obsessively drawn back to the spot. He had returned home and married Malvin's daughter, but his unfulfilled promise ruined him psychologically and materially. He abandoned his old home to head west with his wife and son, but subconsciously circles back to the place which has been the center of his emotional life and is thus his true home. Then and there, Reuben accidentally shoots his own son, a subconscious atonement which ends his emotional paralysis and brings the story's geographical and psychological circles to a joyless close. He will fulfill his promise by burying Malvin's bones, and in that same place he will bury his son. In "Ethan Brand," an obsessed individual also returns to the site of a traumatic event, refigured as a place of death. In fact, something similar recurs in each of Hawthorne's novels and his unfinished romances.

2

"At last, by main strength, I have wrenched and torn an idea out of my miserable brain; or rather, the fragment of an idea, like a tooth ill-drawn, and leaving the roots to torture me," Hawthorne told Charles W. Webber on December 14, 1848, promising to send him a story then entitled "The Unpardonable Sin." Webber had requested an "article" for his projected new magazine, *The New American Review,* and after nearly four dry years, Hawthorne finally had one to send. He must have expected the illustrated monthly literary magazine to prosper, with Webber as editor and the two sons of John James Audubon as his collaborators. Perhaps he also felt he owed a favor to the man who had enthusiastically reviewed *Mosses from an Old Manse* two years before; possibly "Ethan Brand" was Hawthorne's way of answering a question Webber had raised in that review: "Where, out of Hell or Byron, will you find anything to compass the cold, intellectual diabolicism of the infamous Doctor 'Giacomo Rappaccini'?"[13] Hawthorne promised Webber the story only a few days after sending another copy to his sister-in-law Elizabeth Peabody for her *Aesthetic Papers,* probably realizing she would find it too stark. When three months later she requested something less gloomy, he had "Main-street" ready to send her. Meantime, Webber had "The Unpardonable Sin" set in print, and the distinguished artist Felix O. C. Darley carved a powerful woodblock of its climactic scene, in which Ethan Brand stands with upraised arms on top of the fiery kiln.

In completing that story, Hawthorne resumed his identity as a writer. At least six months before his ouster from the Custom House, he had become, as he declared himself in "The Custom-House," "again a literary man." But *The New American Review* was dissolved before its first issue could be distributed, and its printed sheets were placed in storage. In December 1849, just a year after he sent his story to Webber, the little known *Boston Weekly Museum* announced that it would soon publish "an original tale" by Hawthorne. By then Hawthorne was out of a job, but he had continued to produce fiction, and James T. Fields was eager to publish a volume of it. Hawthorne had agreed to let Webber "transfer" "Ethan Brand" to the *Museum,* a periodical he knew nothing about; but he now wanted to publicize his prospective new book while protecting his reputation. Therefore he wanted the *Museum* to specify that Webber – not Hawthorne – had sent them the story, to identify it "as a specimen of a forthcoming book," and to withhold it until that book was ready to market. At that point Hawthorne thought it would be a collection of "Old-Time Legends" including "The Unpardonable Sin," three other new stories, and one that was not yet finished – "The Scarlet Letter." But Fields persuaded him to publish *The Scarlet Letter* as a novel, augmented by "The Custom-House"; and the "forthcoming" collection of shorter works was never published as such.[14] In January 1850, after more than a year of circling – from Hawthorne's desk in Salem to Webber's desk in New York, to a New York storehouse, and then back to Massachusetts– "The Unpardonable Sin" finally made its maiden appearance, misleadingly labeled "For the Boston Weekly Museum" and (as a muddled concession to the author's request) also labeled "From an Unpublished Work."[15]

In March 1851, Hawthorne's friend Evert A. Duyckinck requested and received Hawthorne's permission to publish the story in *The Dollar Magazine,* which he had just purchased, promising a modest payment and suggesting a new title – "Ethan Brand, or, The Unpardonable Sin."[16] Understandably, he was eager to publish a story by the now-celebrated author of *The House of the Seven Gables* and *The Scarlet Letter,* and he had a right to feel proprietary about it. In December 1849, at Webber's request, Duyckinck retrieved the *New American Review* sheets of the story and Darley's woodblock from storage. He sent them to Webber, who sent them on to the *Museum.* Presumably proud of his earlier role, he gave Hawthorne's story the lead position in the May 1851 issue of his new magazine, illustrated by Darley's woodblock, and under the title he had proposed.

In December, the story Hawthorne thought Fields would publish in a collection of "Old-Time Legends," now entitled "Ethan Brand: A Chapter from an Abortive Romance," was finally published by Fields in *The Snow-Image and Other Twice-told Tales,* its third appearance in two years. Predictably, Duyckinck praised the book in his influential fortnightly, *The Literary World,* and another kind of circle was completed.

3

When Hawthorne wrenched "Ethan Brand" out of himself, he did so by imposing on it circularities of plot, setting, and even logic that together constitute an ironic discourse on homecoming.[17] From start to finish, the story interrogates sentimental concepts of home sweet home, and displaces them.

The story begins near the end of Ethan's own story, when he returns to the exact spot where "his search for the Unpardonable Sin" had originated (1051). By returning to the kiln he had left eighteen years before but still calls "my own fireside," he is literally and figuratively completing his fused inner and outer journeys, and he will soon close the larger circle of his life. The narrative develops through repetitive episodes containing orbits of their own. It begins at nightfall with the "new comer" Bartram watching "his" kiln while his little son builds "houses with the scattered fragments of marble" (1051), and it ends the next morning when the kiln's process is completed and father and son see Ethan's skeleton "crumbled into fragments" within it (1066).

Before Ethan climbs up to the "rude, round, tower-like" kiln, preceded by a yet-unattributed roar of laughter, the narrator says "as we have seen," many years had elapsed since he had there conceived the idea of the Unpardonable Sin which "took possession of his life" (1051). Whatever the puzzlement of readers who have "seen" no such thing, they can anticipate catastrophe. The action begins with exchanges between Ethan and Bartram. When Bartram asks "whence come you," Ethan offers a metaphysical reply, describing a completed process: "I come from my search, . . . for, at last, it is finished" (1053). When Bartram asks if he is indeed the man who had sought the Unpardonable Sin, Ethan replies by objectifying himself almost ritually: "He has found what he sought, and therefore he comes back again." And when Bartram probes further, asking "where might it be?" Ethan simply puts his finger on his heart and says "Here!" Then he gives a second laugh,

> as if moved by an involuntary recognition of the infinite absurdity of seeking throughout the world for what was the closest of all things to himself, and looking into every heart, save his own, for what was hidden in no other breast. (1054)

That laugh reverberates among the hills, broadcasting Ethan's ironic self-recognition. He has returned to discover that by his very search, he created what he sought.

We next focus on Bartram, who has sent Joe to summon the villagers and anxiously feels he must deal "heart to heart" with the man who "was making himself at home in his old place" – Bartram's workplace but Ethan's only "place." Their wordless "heart to heart" encounter dramatizes a central trope of "The Haunted Mind" (1835) – "the devils of a guilty heart, that holds its hell within itself" (202):

> The lime-burner's own sins rose up within him, and made his memory riotous with a throng of evil shapes that asserted their kindred with the Master Sin. . . . They were all of one family; they went to and fro between his breast and Ethan Brand's, and carried dark greetings from one to the other. (1055)

Bartram now struggles in horror with a legend about "this strange man" which had once amused him, a legend with its own endlessly repetitive pattern set "in the lurid blaze of this very kiln":

> Before Ethan Brand departed on his search, he had been accustomed to evoke a fiend from the hot furnace of the lime-kiln, night after night, in order to confer with him about the Unpardonable Sin; the Man and the Fiend each laboring to frame the image of some mode of guilt, which could neither be atoned for, nor forgiven. And, with the first gleam of light upon the mountain-top, the fiend crept in at the iron door, there to abide in the intense element of fire, until again summoned forth. (1056)

That legend now invades actuality: When Ethan stoops to open the kiln door, Bartram begs him not to "bring out your devil." After Ethan sternly replies that he was merely trimming the fire and had left the devil "behind on my track," Bartram fearfully asks his final question: "What is the Unpardonable Sin?" Ethan now stands erect and proudly replies,

> "It is a sin that grew within my own breast . . . and nowhere else! The sin of an intellect that triumphed over the sense of brotherhood with man, and reverence for God . . . ! The only sin that deserves a recompense of immortal agony!" (1056–7)

With this vaulting claim, Ethan attains Byronic stature.

The story's middle action begins when the villagers arrive from the tavern, among them three "low and vulgar" men who suggest what Ethan might have become had he never undertaken his

92

search. When his former friends invite him to drink from a bottle which they claim offers "something better . . . than the Unpardonable Sin," he scorns them as "brute beasts." But that very exchange "made him doubt – and, strange to say, it was a painful doubt – whether he had indeed found the Unpardonable Sin, and found it within himself" (1059).

His doubt is dramatized in three consecutive episodes at the center of the story, episodes which range from melodrama through myth to comedy, elaborating the idea of futility through elaborate circle imagery. The first centers on Humphrey, an old man who has wandered around the region for years, asking travelers for news of his daughter Esther. Since Ethan had "been all over the earth," Humphrey assumes he had seen her, "for she makes a grand figure in the world, and everybody goes to see her"; he therefore asks if Esther sent "any word to her old father, or say when she is coming back." In lieu of an answer, Ethan "quailed" before Humphrey as he recalled "the Esther of our tale," the girl he had made "the subject of a psychological experiment, and wasted, absorbed, and perhaps annihilated her soul, in the process." He returns to the present but turns "away from the hoary wanderer" with doubts assuaged, murmuring, "it is no delusion. . . . There is an Unpardonable Sin!" (1060).

Meantime, the story's circularity has been reinforced by the narrator's single sentence about Esther: She had "gone off with a company of circus-performers, . . . and . . . rode on horseback in the ring" (1059). The reader never learns exactly what Ethan did to the "Esther of our tale." Though that phrase recalls the earlier "as we have seen" and the tale's eventual subtitle, "A Chapter From an Abortive Romance," we cannot assume that Hawthorne planned to enclose this story within a larger. As with "Fragments from the Journal of a Solitary Man," the larger work remains metafictional. But that phrase leaves Esther doubly abandoned, forever riding in a ring, a soulless performer who can never come home.

Hawthorne next turns to another homeless performer – an itinerant showman who displays diorama pictures to a "circle of spectators," the villagers who had climbed the hill to see a legendary hero and were disappointed to see only Ethan, a wayfarer who

sat staring into the fire. Therefore they welcomed other amuse-
ment, vicarious travel through a showman's tattered pictures. By
calling the showman "the Jew of Nuremburg," Hawthorne trans-
muted a German he had encountered in the Berkshires into an
archetype of homelessness, the Wandering Jew, whose skepticism
about Jesus doomed him to restless wandering until the Second
Coming. The reader cannot know what Ethan sees when the showman instructs him to look into the diorama, though whatever it
is prompts Ethan to say, "I remember you now." Nor can the
reader know how to interpret the showman's comment, "I find it
to be a heavy matter in my show-box – this Unpardonable Sin!"
But because a youth who had peeped in when Ethan did saw only
"a vacant space of canvas" (1061), it is at least possible that Ethan
also saw only vacancy, an implication that the Unpardonable Sin
had no absolute existence. That would in itself be "heavy matter"
for the Wandering Jew to carry.

Another metaphysical riddle is posed by the narrator's statement
that those who looked into the diorama saw a hand "which might
have been mistaken for the Hand of Destiny, though in truth it
was only the showman's" (1061). The Wandering Jew's circuit
has twice intersected Ethan's, but Hawthorne's "in fact" stresses
human agency. It also raises the issue of authorial control. By
faulting the showman's exhibits as "outrageous scratchings and
daubings ... in a most pitiable condition," Hawthorne seems to
criticize his own story and invite his Ideal Reader's sympathetic
collaboration, as he would soon do in "Main-street" and had often
done before. Only such a reader would willingly suspend disbelief
in Ethan's improbable story yet still see him as a morally responsible agent.

In that story as in Hawthorne's 1838 journal, the showman's
exhibition is immediately followed by another in which the motif
of circling is more literal and ridiculous: A grave old dog suddenly
begins to "run round after his tail, which, to heighten the absurdity
of the proceeding, was a good deal shorter than it should have
been," as if one end of his body was "at deadly and most unfor-
givable enmity with the other," until "as far from the goal as ever,
the foolish old dog ceased his performance" (1062). Like the hypothesis of a blank canvas in the showman's box, the "self-

pursuing dog" suggests that Ethan's goal was delusory. Perhaps Hawthorne – who had disparaged his tale as "the fragment of an idea" – was also admitting something else. Perhaps he saw himself in that "very quiet, well-disposed old dog," who had suddenly roused himself to pursue "an object that could not possibly be attained," in an "effort to amuse the spectators."

Ethan's self-mocking laugh ends the villagers' merriment. In dread that the "awful" sound would reverberate "around the horizon, and that mountain would thunder it to mountain," they "hurried homeward" (1062–3). Bartram and his son also retire, and Ethan remains alone to watch the fire "as in the old time," all the story's dynamism of departure and return concentrated within himself.

His thoughts now amplify and modify what we have previously heard and seen. There will be no more self-mocking laughter, no more eruptions of self-doubt. But his memory is clear. Like Milton's Satan, Dante's damned souls, and Melville's yet unborn Ahab, he can see and name the "place" he left, aware of what he has lost – including his own youthful idealism. But he shows no remorse. He makes no effort to lie, evade the truth, or pervert it. He acknowledges what he has destroyed, his sense of fulfillment unqualified by regret. He has reached the goal he had set for himself, though what he can conceive of himself is a product of monomania.

This review differs from all prior versions of his quest in its far loftier rhetoric:

> Deep within his mind, he was reviewing the gradual, but marvellous change, that had been wrought upon him by the search to which he had devoted himself. He remembered . . . with what reverence he had then looked into the heart of man, viewing it as a temple originally divine, and . . . still to be held sacred by a brother; . . . and prayed that the Unpardonable Sin might never be revealed to him. Then ensued that vast intellectual development, which . . . disturbed the counterpoise between his mind and heart.

Even more melodramatic is his recognition of what ensued when his heart shriveled and died:

> He was now a cold observer, looking on mankind as the subject of his experiment, and, at length, converting man and woman to be

95

his puppets, and pulling the wires that moved them to such degrees
of crime as were demanded for his study.

As master of his own solipsistic universe, "Ethan Brand became
a fiend." But that very awareness now increases his sense of ac-
complishment. Producing the Unpardonable Sin was the "rich,
delicious fruit of his life's labor," he says to himself, and then adds,
"My task is done, and well done!" (1063–4).

Until now all the story's theatrical references have been tied to
recurrence (Esther's as a circus performer, her father's repeated
questions to strangers, the showman's display of his diorama, the
dog's chasing his tail). But the climax of the story – which Darley's
woodblock illustrates – is a one-time-only performance with no
human audience. On the elevated circular stage of the kiln, Ethan
bids farewell to Mother Earth, to mankind, and to the stars of
heaven; he invokes the "deadly element of Fire" to "embrace me
as I do thee" (1065), and plunges bodily into the kiln. As the
story's ultimate ironic return, the man who has tended a kiln which
converts one material into another – marble into lime – ends his
life by converting his own inflexible substance into lime. He may
also be going to an eternal fire, but there is no doubt of his "homecoming" to Mother Earth, in the form of inert matter.

From the start, his idea of home has been devoid of all intimacy:
There is no one to welcome him, and nowhere to rest his head.
In no other character and in no other story did Hawthorne more
starkly define a disjunction between individual and community or
between head and heart. Ethan Brand has none of the traditional
attributes of home – no parental house or forefather's graves, no
identity as a son, husband, or father. Although no one else in the
tale has a traditional family – Joe's mother is presumably dead,
and the daughter of the presumably wifeless Humphrey is a run-
away – Ethan is radically self-isolated, someone who thinks only
of himself and would never follow a father's footsteps or anyone
else's. He returns to the kiln not for shelter or protection but simply
as a form of completion. Within his self-enclosed universe he has
moved along his chosen path to complete a self-defined task. His
identity, like legends about him, is coeval with his search and
eventual certainty that he and he alone has found the Unpardonable Sin. His only mother is Mother Earth, his only father the God

he displaced, and we know of no woman in his life but the one he has "wasted." For the man who had trampled on the "great heart" of mankind, there can be no friend but the "deadly element of Fire." His last words — "Embrace me as I do thee!" — pervert the rhetoric of friendship and familiarity. Bounded by mortality, he completes a final circular trajectory. The story that began when he mounted the hill to his "own fireside" ends when he mounts to its top and leaps in. Although Oberon in "Fragments from the Journal of a Solitary Man" could anticipate a grave near his parents', and although the narrator warns Wakefield that a grave is the only home that awaits him, Ethan denies himself even that kind of home.

But before completing Ethan's story, Hawthorne metaphorically offers the reader an intimation of heaven, a concession to popular taste but also an expression of his own perennial hope:

> Stepping from one to another of the clouds that rested in the hills, and thence to the loftier brotherhood that sailed in air, it seemed almost as if a mortal man might ascend into the heavenly regions. Earth was so mingled with sky that it was a daydream to look at it.

Then the "familiar and homely" is asserted through a stagecoach horn, which sets off a concert of "elaborate harmony" as each of the "great hills" surrounding the kiln contributes its own "strain of airy sweetness" (1066). In the eyes and ears of little Joe (the ideal homebody whose father fears he has too much of his mother in him, and who anticipates Ernest in "The Great Stone Face") the world rejoices now that "the strange man is gone." But the story's final image is a graphic announcement of his ultimate homecoming: In the heart-hearth of his kiln, "the relics of Ethan were crumbled into fragments" (1067).

Ethan's quest was not for fame or fortune but knowledge of the Unpardonable Sin, a sin so heinous that it was beyond even God's mercy to pardon it. That search constitutes Ethan's identity and his legendary fame. He returns to the point where his search originated, his only home, a success in his own terms despite a few eruptions of doubt; and that very success also defines his human failure, his separation from all human connection except as a detached puppetmaster. Never had Hawthorne so concertedly disrupted the traditional ideas of home (including home as haven and as vocation), or so starkly defined the self-reifying impulse that drove Ethan away from home and then back.

Ethan invented himself, though Hawthorne invented Ethan, drawing on his own huge repertoire of feelings about home and about returning home to Salem. He created a story of insistent returns and reversions, filled with episodes, and implications within episodes, which have orbits of their own. But he kept his focus on a wanderer who imposed meaning on his life by moving purposefully around the world and then returning. Apart from the question of whether there really was an Unpardonable Sin and (if so) whether it really grew only in Ethan's heart, his commitment to his own circling path has a heroic if horrific absurdity. The logic of his quest is inherently paradoxical: To seek sin is to become embroiled in it and destroyed by it, albeit willfully destroyed. Ethan imposed a design on his life which defined his life as a loop he finally erased. He controlled his own plot, ignoring villagers who sought only to distract themselves through inebriation or entertainment.

Through Ethan Brand, a man with no human ties and no home but the kiln he had worked, Hawthorne objectified his deepest anxieties about his birthplace, his self-isolating vocation, and mortality itself. Though he did not lay his problems to rest, he temporarily corralled them. Out of his anxieties about homecoming came the narrative pattern of his story: a circular pattern with complex variations. From the moment we hear Ethan's roar of laughter at the bottom of the hill, Hawthorne provokes expectations in the reader which each successive episode intensifies, complicates, and emphatically fulfills. Ethan climbs the hill at the beginning of Hawthorne's story and goes even higher before his ultimate downfall, a rise and fall that close the larger circle of his self-defined life. He is a "stranger" encountered at nightfall who dies before morning, an image Hawthorne amplifies by intimating heavenly approval of earthly harmony. Ethan's homecoming is thematized as inevitable but joyless. Severed from antecedents and denied all possibility of descendants, he can live only in legends –

those the villagers tell, and this one. By telling about a man who faced the worst, Hawthorne empowered himself to keep on writing.

NOTES

1 Nathaniel Hawthorne, *The Letters, 1843–1853,* ed. Thomas Woodson et al. (Columbus: Ohio State University Press, 1985), p. 251. See Lea Newman, *A Reader's Guide to the Short Stories of Nathaniel Hawthorne* (Boston: G. K. Hall, 1979), pp. 95–112, for succinct summaries of the publication history, sources, and criticism of "Ethan Brand."

2 Nathaniel Hawthorne, *The Scarlet Letter,* in *Novels,* ed. Millicent Bell (New York: The Library of America, 1983), pp. 126, 128–9.

3 He loved his mother despite that coldness, he noted in his journal on July 29, 1849, when his deep grief at her imminent death took him by surprise. Nathaniel Hawthorne, *The American Notebooks,* ed. Claude M. Simpson (Columbus: Ohio State University Press, 1972), p. 429.

4 Gloria C. Erlich, *Family Themes and Hawthorne's Fiction: The Tenacious Web* (Rutgers: Rutgers University Press, 1984), pp. 75–6.

5 *Novels,* p. 141.

6 *Novels,* pp. 155, 156, 157.

7 Hawthorne, *Notebooks,* pp. 86–151. He was then still living in the Manning house in Salem, though the following winter he would move to Boston and become inspector of the Custom House there.

8 *Notebooks,* p. 251.

9 *The Poetics of Enchantment* (Ithaca: Cornell University Press, 1977), p. 147. Dryden rightly observes that Hawthorne's fiction is "filled with homeless characters who seek recognition and reconciliation," though Ethan Brand's search is unique.

10 Page references to Hawthorne's tales given parenthetically are from Nathaniel Hawthorne, *Tales and Sketches,* ed. Roy Harvey Pearce (New York: The Library of America, 1982).

11 *Notebooks,* p. 429.

12 Oberon is the nickname Hawthorne used in letters to Horatio Bridge during his "twelve lonely years" after graduating from Bowdoin College.

13 The anonymous review which appeared in the September 1846 issue of the *American Whig Review* (4:296–316) is reprinted in J. Donald Crowley, *Hawthorne: The Critical Heritage* (New York: Barnes and Noble, 1970), pp. 126–34.

14 Though Fields's argument prevailed a few days later, as late as January 15, 1850, Hawthorne expected to include "The Scarlet Letter" in a book called "Old-Time Legends; together with *sketches, experimental and ideal.*" *Letters*, pp. 305–6.

15 *Letters*, pp. 300–1; *Boston Weekly Museum*, 2:234–5.

16 *The Dollar Magazine*, 7:193–201; *Letters*, pp. 404–5. Five years before, Duyckinck had done Hawthorne good service by arranging for the publication of *Mosses from an Old Manse.*

17 Many of these circular motifs have been discussed by Richard Harter Fogle in *Hawthorne's Fiction: The Light and the Dark* (Norman: University of Oklahoma Press, 1965), pp. 41–58, and Kermit Vanderbilt in "The Unity of Hawthorne's 'Ethan Brand'" (*College English*, 24 [1963]: 453–6).

Historicizing Hell in Hawthorne's Tales

DAVID LEVERENZ

1

"WHAT do you think of my becoming an Author, and relying for support upon my pen," Hawthorne wrote to his mother in 1821, as he was preparing to enter Bowdoin College. "Indeed I think the illegibility of my handwriting is very authorlike." Ostentatiously he has just considered and rejected the obvious professions: a minister would be "so dull . . . A Puddle of Water," half the lawyers starve, physicians live by the diseases and deaths of their patients. Now the young man archly signals his desire for literary fame. "How proud you would feel to see my works praised by the reviewers, as equal to proudest productions of the scribbling sons of John Bull."

With a curious alliterative slippage, from "proud" mother to "praised" works to "proudest productions" of English contemporaries, Hawthorne imagines his mother reading not his future writings but his reviews. In Hawthorne's mind, becoming an Author with a capital A is filial, rivalrous, and ultimately colonial. It depends on his ability to match "the scribbling sons" of English literature. More practically, it means pleasing the reviewers, who will assess his writings in relation to English cultural traditions.

As he considers the condition of authors in New England, he evokes the truly Hawthornian swerve, at once flippant, ironic, and exposed: "But Authors are always poor Devils, and therefore Satan may take them."[1] Here Hawthorne seems to speak with the voice of his future readers, in a country where only Washington Irving had been able to make a living by "relying for support upon [his] pen." A dismissive cliché, "poor Devils," conjures up his countrymen's contempt for leisured imaginations. Writers are idlers, a view Hawthorne frequently toys with in his prefaces, and idle hands are the Devil's plaything. Yet Hawthorne turns readerly closure into a breezy writerly openness: "therefore Satan may take them." The statement twists several contradictory ways, ostensibly toward authors, implicitly toward readers. A writer plays with witchcraft, the imagination can be possessed by plots and passions, Old Deluder Satan is the Father of Lies. These issues had helped to constitute the neoclassic ideals of rationality, and they would bedevil Hawthorne's own ambivalence about the solitary creative mind.[2] At the same time, "them" has an edge turning outward, anticipating Hawthorne's relish for satire veiled as self-exploration.

From "My Kinsman, Major Molineux" (1831) to "Feathertop" (1852), Hawthorne plays variations on the theme of "Satan may take them." Male protagonists in particular discover that " 'myself am Hell' " (*Paradise Lost*, IV, 75). The Devil actually hisses inside one protagonist's selfishness throughout most of "Egotism, or, the Bosom Serpent" (1843), until a self-sacrificing wife makes the serpent disappear. In "The Haunted Mind" (1834), a solitary man's seemingly innocuous reverie about nocturnal dozing begets a ghastly fever of self-revelation that can afflict any mind at midnight: "the devils of a guilty heart, that holds its hell within itself." For such "horror of the mind," only the thought of a tender woman's influence can bring peace (202–3).[3]

If conventionally tenderized women relieve men from the dangers of getting to know themselves, the Satanic resolutions go just the other way, expanding the threat. They make Hawthorne sound remarkably Calvinistic, as Melville was the first to celebrate. A psychological critic could find several levels of rage, alienation, and self-hatred in Hawthorne's fascination with hellfire, or for that matter with fires of any kind. A social historian could situate Hawthorne's uses of Hell in an equally long tradition of haughty, agonized, and vengeful jeremiads, of which Dante's *Inferno* is surely the finest example. In that tradition, Hell voices the rage, disdain, and imperious despair of a high-status group being exiled from power by what one recent social historian of religion has called "the rude hand of innovation."[4] To combine these two perspectives, Hawthorne's own ironic historicizing of Puritan Calvinism could itself be historicized as an elitist reaction formation: at once a guarded satire of his nation's bourgeoisie in the making, and an exploration of his own imaginative deviance in a normatively manly age.

But who can trust Satan, formerly a spectral liar, now an antiquated fraud? By the 1830s, "Old Deluder Satan" had become a threadbare bogeyman, not to be taken seriously by enlightened cosmopolitans who had jettisoned a Calvinist God for a nurturing Christ.[5] "In modern times Satan, if not a figure of speech, is at least a distant or intangible force," Francis Henry Underwood writes in an 1887 appreciation of Hawthorne, the only nineteenth-century account to pay any attention to his quaint and curious devils. Underwood, who seems to have invented the phrase "New England Renaissance," attributes Hawthorne's preoccupation with Satan and Hell to the unfortunate shadow of his Puritan past, and there, for the most part, historicizing Hawthorne's Hell has rested.[6] Richard H. Brodhead, one of his most astute recent critics, takes care to differentiate the premodernist complexities of "daimoni-zation" from Hawthorne's creaky demons.[7]

Historicizing Hell in Hawthorne's tales has to begin by focusing on the curious lack of legitimacy, or authority, that his reader-sensitive narratives grant to their theological resolutions. The tales frequently culminate with gloomily abstracted truths about the hellfires of evil lurking in human subjectivity, especially in young male loners. Yet these truths provide several kinds of exits from their proclamations of guilt. The moral lessons appear in an aging genre, allegory, that readers tended to resist.[8] Moreover, the preacher is the world's first snake-oil salesman, from whom readers felt comfortably or uneasily detached. The readerly process resembles what Gregory Vlastos has recently argued for Socrates, a "complex irony" throwing readers back on their own freedom to interpret, like it or not, with a Hawthornian twist. Readers end in the same self-scrutinizing solitude that exposed the protagonist's receptivity to Satan.[9] Did Young Goodman Brown dream a wild dream? "Be it so, if you will" (288).

"Satan may take them" therefore orients yet disorients expectations for interpretive stability. If Satan's accusations of secret guilt nettle the mind with shame, Satan's narrative status perplexes the mind into doubt. How can these climactic allegorical moments constitute both truth and delusion at the same time? Such indeterminacy is what I want to historicize in this essay.

At the start of his literary career, Hawthorne writes "colonial allegories" in a postcolonial country on the international periphery of capitalist transformations. The United States was still a dispersed assemblage of farms, artisan villages, and mercantile city-towns, separated by an ocean from European political tensions and cultural greatness. Fresh from two wars with England yet united more by English traditions than by a hated enemy, having neither a powerful central government nor a large central city to magnetize national and cultural coherence, the country derived its ambiguous unity of states from regional mixtures of Anglo-Continental immigrant heritages and a diffusely dynamic ideology of economic expansion, in which elite civic leadership uneasily abetted various kinds of entrepreneurial competition and mobilities.

Recent new historicist criticism of Hawthorne has tended to presume a national production of ideology – whether liberal, patriarchal, or middle class – that does not become hegemonic until after the Civil War.[10] Hawthorne's roots were local, in the Florentine mode; he thought of himself as a citizen of Concord or Salem, exiled even at home, as he notes in "The Custom-House." Yet from the beginning of his career he focuses on the past and present manhood of the region already defining the course of American expansion. Authorizing his subject through allegory, Hawthorne depends on Bunyan and Spenser – his two favorite authors since childhood – and to a lesser extent on Dante, to probe and shame his countrymen. His stories deauthorize their allegorical shamings by exposing the untenably colonial status of their narrators.

Sacvan Bercovitch has called Hawthorne's mid-century romance narrations, especially *The Scarlet Letter*, a "thick propaganda" for a consensus ideology of American liberalism, and that's partly right.[11] More comprehensively, Hawthorne's narrations can be called "thick ventriloquism." They mime yet undermine the relocation of public authority in New England from a postcolonial elite, defined through Eurocentric status hierarchy, to a new middle class whose rhetoric dichotomizes male self-reliance and female self-sacrifice. If Hawthorne moves from what I call colonial allegory to what he eventually called "psychological romance," the shift signals his ventriloquistic realignment as New England becomes a capitalist core for the production of goods and meanings.

In other words, Hawthorne finally discovered the difference between Anglophilic reviewers and the New England market. To explore the full consequences of that shift, he had to move beyond allegories about men obsessed with discovering and controlling meaning. His romances venture into more profoundly risky narrations of female self-reliance in conflict with the power relations that construct male and female subjectivities. At that point, "Satan may take them" shifts from a climactic plotting device to a more intermittent, gender-neutral way of dramatizing tensions between desire and self-control. The trope loses much of its urgency as a self-deauthorizing response to the social transformation of meanings for authority and subjectivity – what Michael McKeon has called "the problem of mediation."[12]

2

"My Kinsman, Major Molineux," Hawthorne's first experiment in using "Satan may take them" as a double-edged sword, dramatizes his country's transformation from agrarian communities based on kinship and deference to an urban economy encouraging upward mobility through self-reliance. Hawthorne depicts the change as a journey into Hell. This reading is well known. Not until the narration's deferential kinship with Dante's *Inferno* has been acknowledged, however, do the story's colonial contradictions become part of the meaning-making. A tale ostensibly shaming Hawthorne's countrymen depends on a high theological allegory for allusions which deauthorize the narrator's moral indignation.

Toward the end of "My Kinsman," Robin sees for the third time the man whose fiery eyes, "double prominence" on his forehead, and "parti-colored features" have already been linked to "devils" and "fiends" (72, 78). Now the man is on horseback leading a great crowd, amid "a redder light" and "a band of fearful wind-instruments, sending forth a fresher discord" (84). The hellish leader thunders a halt; "the trumpets vomited a horrid breath, and held their peace; the shouts and laughter of the people died away, and there remained only an universal hum, nearly allied to silence."[13]

That extraordinarily nuanced phrase, "nearly allied," evokes the closeness, the detachment, and the eeriness of the not-quite-silenced atmosphere, as well as the political alliances not quite openly revealed, prefigured in the multiple meanings for the leader's "parti-colored features." Robin, too, has been eager for a party. Once before he has heard "a trumpet." Then he "wistfully" interprets the wind instruments and the "wild and confused" laughter as " 'some prodigious merrymaking' " (83). Now all the parties converge: the leader's factionalized face, the political overthrow of authority imposed from England, and the carnivalesque merrymaking. Robin's bold reductiveness does constitute shrewdness, a word originally signifying demonic possession, as he lets the party carry the heavy symbolic freight of what the narrator allegorizes as an unresolvable psychological split between rebellion and "mourning" in a national coming of age from kinship dependency to self-reliant independence. Discarding his useless Anglophilic connections, Robin takes on an upwardly mobile identity "nearly allied" to an ascendent culture of political parties.

A simple way to historicize this moment would be to focus on the changing meanings of the word "party" in the 1820s and 1830s. In *The Transformation of Political Culture*, Ronald P. Formisano details the decline of deferential networking as the function of party politics in Massachusetts, and the rise of mass parties by 1840 – the first in the world. The eighteenth-century connotations of the word, "parties to a dispute or a disagreement," had been linked to a corporate society of close-knit towns and relatively stable elite leadership, though anyone pretending to too much aristocratic grandeur, notably Governor Gore in 1809, was speedily defeated. By the 1840s, the Whigs and the Democrats had become ends in themselves. Patriotic invocations of the Revolutionary War, not deference to virtuous civic leadership, became the customary Fourth-of-July rhetoric to fictionalize national consensus.[14]

In the late 1820s and early 1830s, political life was in such turmoil that a new party had to be formed to re-appropriate the progressive center from the fading Federalist elite. If the Whigs, founded in 1834, represented a nation-building core, the Democrats represented what Formisano calls "the Periphery's ancient resistance to the 'haughty' culture and morality of the Core and the political or economic domination of the Center." But that dichotomy is too simple. When John O'Sullivan founded the *Democratic Review* in 1837, Hawthorne's future friend – who coined the phrase "Manifest Destiny" – invited him to contribute to a journal that would be "taking *ton* of the first class in England for model."[15] One suspects that O'Sullivan already knew his man. "First class" English tone, not political manifestoes, would secure Hawthorne's interest.

Hawthorne used Democratic friends such as Franklin Pierce, Jonathan Cilley, and O'Sullivan for that most ancient of political reasons, connections. These long-term friendships helped secure one half of Hawthorne's public persona, as man of the world. Being a Democrat nearly allied to patrician Boston also entitled him to a position of doubleness, speaking from the periphery of political change yet complicit with patronage, in the party but not of it. As Francis Underwood would write, trying to explain Hawthorne's admiring campaign biography of Pierce, a Bowdoin classmate elected President in 1852: "The social aristocracy was then generally Whig; the anti-slavery men were apart in a respectable minority; and a pro-slavery democrat, such as Hawthorne avowed himself, was held in abhorrence by both the other parties."[16] Always the outsider, Hawthorne writes his first great tale to historicize his country's progress toward political parties with detached allegorical disdain.

But what about that trumpet? The specifically Dantean allusions are easy to miss, partly because the narrator makes such high allegorical meaning out of Dante's one dirty joke. At the end of Canto 21 of the *Inferno,* Dante and Virgil are edging along the eighth circle (fraud), fifth pouch (barratry). Malacoda orders Barbariccia and ten subordinate devils to guide Dante and Virgil around the bubbling stew of pitch, where tarred sinners struggle with their eternal punishment for graft. Grinding their teeth in rage, the ten devils set out, but not before each gives his leader a Bronx cheer, pressing his tongue between his teeth as a wind instrument.

As for Barbariccia, in the line that ends the canto, "ed elli avea del cul fatto trombetta." Just listen to the sounds! As Allen Mandelbaum translates it, "And he had made a trumpet of his ass." Or, in the 1867 translation of Hawthorne's friend Longfellow: "And he had made a trumpet of his rump." Or in the 1822 Henry Cary translation that Hawthorne read aloud to his wife during their first year together,

> ... each
> Had first between his teeth prest close the tongue,
> Toward their leader for a signal looking,
> Which he with sound obscene triumphant gave.[17]

Making sure that no one misses it, Dante takes the first twelve lines of Canto 22 to consider Barbariccia's originality. Musingly he concludes, in Allen Mandelbaum's translation, "never yet have I seen ... so strange a bugle!" Longfellow's strong misreading catches the grotesqueness by calling it a "bagpipe." Twice emphasizing the trumpets that "vomited a horrid breath" and the fearfully discordant wind instruments, Hawthorne may have risked an oblique but unmistakable allusion to Barbariccia's fart, especially if a Bowdoin classmate had told him about the Italian version. More certainly, he evokes Dante's obscene leader and those bad-breath devils.[18]

If this scene specifically evokes Dante's Canto 21, not just Milton's Pandemonium, that means we have to take other parallels to Canto 21 more seriously, particularly the guide, the pitch, and the fraud. The ambiguously kind gentleman, for instance, has been generally linked to Spenser's Archimago or to Virgil leading Dante through a vaguely Dantean Hell.[19] By Canto 23, Dante's Virgil has become a "mirror" and a "mother" to the mid-life soul-traveler, counterpointing the growing frozenness of heart that becomes permanent in the bottom circle of Hell. Unlike Virgil's good mothering, the mentoring of Robin's guide consists primarily of his quiet observation, " 'May not one man have several voices, Robin, as well as two complexions?' " (83). In choosing to " 'rise in the world' " by accepting a crowd-based adult identity, Robin chooses a party-voiced devil as his guide. Already Robin has almost discarded his last name of Molineux; his new last name will be legion.

So far, neither my method nor my conclusion is new. I have been playing the oldest literary game, source hunting, to support a conservative political reading. At best it leads us down the road one critic started to take until he recoiled, saying in effect, that's impossible; Hawthorne was a Democrat.[20] The Dante connection encourages us to historicize the tale as a High Tory indictment of lower-class leaders. Under the guise of narrating a slightly displaced account of the American Revolution, Hawthorne has used an animus "nearly allied" to Dante's revenge against the "new men" of Florence who exiled him.

What makes the intertextual link to Canto 21 much more unsettling is the Canto's "contrapasso," the punishment that fits the sin. The Canto depicts barrators covered from head to toe, like Major Molineux, in tarry pitch. Flaxman's Dante has a drawing of the scene.[21] Though the narrator commands his readers to feel tragic pity for the besieged colonial governor as a man caught between overseas tyranny and mob rule, the Dantean parallel implies that Robin's humiliated kinsman has either gained his position by fraud or has been selling favors, since the first meaning of "barratry" is the purchase or sale of an office in church or state.

If Robin's kinsman *deserves* to be in Hell, a reading wholly unavailable from the story and dependent on its status as colonial allegory in several ways – it also links Major Molineux with Prime Minister Robert Walpole's "Robinocracy" and the nepotistic Governor Thomas Hutchinson – then the narrator's insistence on demonic associations for everyone else seems undecidably reliable yet unreliable.[22] Authority itself, like kinship, self-deconstructs into what Milton's Satan calls "the hateful siege / Of contraries" (*Paradise Lost*, IX, 121–2). Either the Dantean allusions contradict each other or, what may be worse, they collude to rob the narrator of any moral force. His moral vindictiveness – "trampling all on an old man's heart" (86) – seems the inverse side of Robin's amoral laughter. Closure, like kinship, cannot be secured.

"I am not quite sure that I entirely comprehend my own meaning in some of these blasted allegories," Hawthorne wrote to his publisher in 1854.[23] He seems to have been especially wary of "My Kinsman." Publishing it anonymously in 1831 in *The Token* (dated 1832), as "by the Author of Sights from a Steeple," Hawthorne left it unauthored and untouched for twenty years, while *Twice-Told Tales* and *Mosses from an Old Manse* established his reputation as a short story writer. Only in 1851, when the success of *The Scarlet Letter* prompted his publisher to hound him for a quick story collection, did he let Fields and Ticknor ransack old magazines for tales he had clearly forgotten. Presumably the last to be found, "My Kinsman" comes at the tail end of *The Snow-Image and Other Tales*, along with a prefatory letter saying he was "disposed to quarrel" with these "trifles," "early windfalls" with "so many faults."[24] In a friendly review, E. A. Duyckinck said the story was a bad "joke": "most lame and impotent conclusion."[25]

Not until 1951, when an essay by Q. D. Leavis lavished praise on the story, did anyone begin to think "My Kinsman" was significant. As Nina Baym has observed, it was the Freudians who made the tale a masterpiece.[26] The canonization of its ambivalence happened in the 1950s, a decade celebrating "the end of ideology," when the allegory's antinational satire could be subsumed in an analysis of a representative young man's complex psychology. For one hundred years the story lay dormant, the sleeping beauty of the American canon, until kissed by an English queen.

Hawthorne's recoil from his first experiment in colonial allegory can probably be attributed more to its antipatriotic bite than to its Dantean contradictions. "My Kinsman" differs from almost all his later tales in adopting a narrative voice quietly but explicitly at odds with his New England readers on the very issue that would most make them bristle: the sacred, nation-making cause of the American Revolution. Clearly, in the absence of aristocratic patronage, antipatriotic meaning-making could not be his route to literary fame, though he prudently displaced the story's setting to Boston in the 1730s. Dropping what amounts to a thoroughly contradictory attempt to use colonial allegory for social satire and psychological exploration, Hawthorne began to experiment with more ventriloquistic narrations of the Satan-susceptible self.

3

From the beginning of his literary career, Hawthorne's narrations construct a morally trustworthy voice as the reader's guide and representative. His "I" is also a "we," judiciously assessing the Satan-susceptible heart. By the 1840s Hawthorne was succeeding so well at his readerly ventriloquism that contemporary reviewers enthusiastically celebrate his style for its purity and serenity — "we are soothed," wrote Poe.[27] Since such responses seem incomprehensible to modern readers alienated from Hawthorne's conventions of narrative naturalness, a substantial critical tradition has focused on the question of his narrator's reliability. Trust the tale, not the teller, D. H. Lawrence urged as early as 1923. Nina Baym has expressed astonishment that Hawthorne could work so hard, especially in the Sketches, at complying with his readers, far beyond what the market required; it amounted to self-repression.[28]

Hawthorne himself broadly hints that such narrations pleasure his readers by removing any danger of solitary introspection. Dichotomizing self and society in his preface to the 1851 edition of *Twice-Told Tales,* he writes ironically of what he sacrificed to fashion his popular Sketches, namely, idiosyncrasy and individuality as well as deep thought. Their style is never "profound"; it also lacks "abstruseness" and "obscurity," traits "which mark the written communications of a solitary mind with itself. . . . It is, in fact, the style of a man of society. Every sentence, so far as it embodies thought or sensibility, may be understood and felt by anybody[.]" This is clearly not the best kind of writing, Hawthorne concludes. "They are not the talk of a secluded man with his own mind and heart, (had it been so, they could hardly have failed to be more deeply and permanently valuable,) but his attempts . . . to open an intercourse with the world" (1152).[29]

If we trust that the teller is part of the tale, then a similar dichotomy becomes crucial to Hawthorne's complex irony. Using the seeming authority of a gentlemanly, sociable, reasonably moral man of the world to interrogate a dangerously isolated, potentially Satan-susceptible imagination, Hawthorne subtly undermines the interpretive stability of New England's masculine gender constructions, old and new. Both narrator and protagonist seem symbiotically inauthentic, except as they constitute an indeterminate tension of sympathy and accusation. One is too pleasantly accommodating and deferential, yet intermittently judgmental; the other

111

is too self-capitalizing, a "man of adamant," yet delusively driven by dreams gone wild.

An early, conventionally romantic version of the doubling, "The Devil in Manuscript" (1835), can be contrasted with two other tales from that year, "Young Goodman Brown" and "Wakefield," to show how Hawthorne developed reliable yet unreliable narration to mimic and undermine the moral authority of gentlemanly readers. To borrow from Michael McKeon's discussion of allegory and mediation in *The Origins of the English Novel,* the tales use allegory to ward off the potential degeneration of shared meanings into what McKeon calls "individual self-interest and capitalist self-service."[30] Within the allegorical construction of meanings, devils serve as climactic devices to establish both an historical moral truth – the shameful human heart – and an all too historical inauthenticity – the sociable narrator, who attempts to mediate between precapitalist status constructions of the gentleman and an emerging entrepreneurial ideology of self-reliance.

"The Devil in Manuscript" seems to have been part of an unpublished sequence of stories about Oberon, the melancholy king of prankster magic in Shakespeare's *Midsummer Night's Dream* and Hawthorne's self-chosen nickname at Bowdoin. It quickly disintegrates into a mawkish mixture of self-loathing, rage at publishers, and fitful satire, probably akin to the "half savage, half despairing" mood in which Hawthorne had burned his own early stories.[31] Told by an anonymous "I," one of Hawthorne's early experiments in man-of-the-world narrators, the tale presents Oberon as a writer about to burn his witchcraft manuscripts. While Oberon questions whether his writings or his " 'conception' " embody " 'the character of a fiend' " (330–1), or whether the Devil lurks in the seventeen booksellers who have returned his manuscripts, the narrator privately corroborates the judgment of the market: "His tales would make a more brilliant appearance in the fire than anywhere else" (332–3). The narrator's detached urbanity punctures Oberon's maudlin posturing about what tortures Dante might contrive for bad authors. Finally, as Oberon burns his manuscripts, he sees the fiend amid the flames, though the narrator sees nothing but burning papers. Then shouts come from outside: Several roofs are ablaze. The story ends with Oberon's hysterical cry: " 'Here I stand — a triumphant author! Huzza! Huzza! My brain has set the town on fire! Huzza!' " (337).

It may be a measure of how poorly Hawthorne regarded "My Kinsman, Major Molineux" that he republished it with this story in *The Snow-Image*. Both the self-doubt and the rage at the literary marketplace seem embarrassingly sophomoric. Nonetheless, "The Devil in Manuscript" points to many of Hawthorne's recurrent narrative issues: a split between uncomprehending men of society and self-vexing solitary minds, a fascination with New England demonism, an oscillation between readerly and writerly perspectives, the ambiguous use of "Satan may take them" for what amounts here to both social satire and self-satire.

Set in that frame, "Young Goodman Brown" and "Wakefield" constitute a diptych. Published within a month of each other in 1835, they consolidate a long American tradition that had already begun with "Rip Van Winkle," the story of a man cutting adrift from intimacy, sometimes returning to domesticity and sometimes not. The tradition shapes narratives from Melville's *Moby Dick* to Russell Banks's *Continental Drift*. Dashiell Hammett's *The Maltese Falcon* even incorporates a transposition of "Wakefield" as its "auxiliary heart," Richard Brodhead's fine phrase for a tale within a tale. If Hawthorne's narrator repeatedly mocks the "crafty smile" (292, 298) flitting about the face of the "crafty nincompoop" (294), Sam Spade momentarily breaks his laconic habits to tell the uncomprehending Miss Wonderly, his own Una/Duessa, a seemingly irrelevant story about "Charlie Flitcraft." Charlie inexplicably left one wife and life to marry another woman in another city simply because a near-accident brought him face to face with the randomness of the universe, and he wanted to adjust to it.[32] Hawthorne's tale, like most of the texts in the tradition, offers considerably less clarity about motive. Huck Finn's antiallegorical response to *Pilgrim's Progress*, one of the two or three ur-texts, sums up the tradition: "about a man who left his family it didn't say why."[33]

Both "Young Goodman Brown" and "Wakefield" are about exactly that. Both tales also dramatize an unresolvable tension between inscrutable loners and judgmental narrators, who progress from the postcolonial stability of Spenserian allegory

("Young Goodman Brown") or London social status ("Wake-field") through increasingly strenuous accusations of their doubles, as they keep trying for dear life to hold on to some kind of moral authority. The delusive sense of closure and counterclosure at the end of each story seems specious, in part because each narrator tries to make male self-reliance the Devil's plaything. "Young Goodman Brown" flagrantly climaxes with Satan, who makes a cameo appearance in the last line of "Wakefield," as "the Outcast of the Universe" (298) – Milton's Lucifer being the first such Outcast.

Hawthorne's two representations of Satanic self-reliance sharply contrast in meaning as well as staging. One proclaims universal guilt, and the narrator seems half to agree. The other signifies not human evil but the absolute meaninglessness awaiting anyone who steps aside from his social place. Yet the two morals share a melodramatic allegorical abstractedness waving a red flag of fictionality over the closure of authoritative truths. If each ending seems morally intense yet evasively packaged, the latent linkage of devils also suggests a link between narrators, notably in their uses of allegorical judgments to license their shaming of socially uncompliant men. Each tries to reduce the threat of self-reliance to traditional social virtue by making the isolated self seem both dangerous and powerless. Only absolute meaninglessness or absolute evil could make a man want a room or a gloom of his own.

If each narrator tries to make moral meaning by shaming his protagonist, each also stages his allegory with ironic intertextual theatrics. The urbane, faceless, nameless narrator of "Wakefield" affirms his "we" by staging Wakefield as a piece of "whim wham" (294) in which the narrator plays author, director, and sole audience. "Now for a scene!" (295). Wakefield's very name is mockingly literary, transforming the pastoral patriarch of Oliver Goldsmith's *Vicar of Wakefield* into a contemptible spectacle of urban deviance and marital irresponsibility. The crafty narrator both acknowledges and disowns his crafty double: "We know, each for himself, that none of us would perpetrate such a folly, yet feel as if some other might" (290). That half buried rumination, "each for himself," surfaces in the last paragraph as a dichotomy: Either "individuals are so nicely adjusted to a system, and systems to one another, and to a whole," or, "by stepping aside for a moment, a man exposes himself to a fearful risk of losing his place forever" (298).

Ostensibly the "fearful risk" is of losing one's place or, as he says earlier, "reciprocal influence" (297). Yet the dichotomy subtly shifts the production of subjectivity from "nicely adjusted" to "a man exposes himself," just as Wakefield's "stepping aside" has created his uniqueness, whereas his stepping back in stops the narrator's imagination at the threshold. Moreover, the final sentence disorients rather than fulfills the narrator's initial assurance "that there will be a pervading spirit and a moral, . . . done up neatly, and condensed into the final sentence" (290–1). The suddenly expansive otherness of "the Outcast of the Universe" sounds monstrously yet wistfully romantic, as if the narrator, like Blake's Milton, were of the Devil's party without knowing it. After all, from the beginning Wakefield comes to life only as a collective imagining: "We are free to shape out our own idea, and call it by his name" (291).

The other narrator, an equally nameless and faceless but more provincial finger-wagger, similarly disowns and indicts his double, Young Goodman Brown. If Wakefield has a "morbid vanity" (293), a "cold" heart (291), and a "feeble" mind (293, 296) as well as that "crafty smile," Young Goodman Brown quickly displays an "evil purpose" that soon makes him "the chief horror of the scene" (276, 284). He is worse than the Devil himself: "All through the haunted forest, there could be nothing more frightful than the figure of Goodman Brown" (284). Hectoring this "demoniac" severely from first to last, the narrator shows more sympathy for the Devil than for his protagonist. If Satan enters as a Spenserian Archimago figure, a delusive tempter, he is also a knowledgeably demystifying historian, citing verifiable cruelties of Puritans to Quaker women and Indians.

At the climax, Satan becomes the agonized Lucifer who opens *Paradise Lost*, still thrice capable of tears amid the "darkness visible," or rather, as the narrator puts it, "almost sad, . . . as if his once angelic nature could yet mourn for our miserable race." The narrator has already anticipated Lucifer's pronouncements about human " 'nature.' " If Lucifer declares that the human heart is a

" 'fountain...which inexhaustibly supplies more evil impulses than human power – than my power, at its utmost! – can make manifest in deeds' " (287), the narrator has said the same thing: "The fiend in his own shape is less hideous, than when he rages in the breast of man" (284).

As various critics have argued, the story ends in an ironic, antiallegorical mode. Interpretation novelistically opens out to pluralistic, skeptical readers at Young Badman Brown's expense. A chastened skepticism about moral skepticism, or a psychological investigation of a young man's sexual nervousness, or an ironic historicizing of Puritans who believed in spectral evidence – these readings offer contradictory hopes of interpretive stability.[34] It must have been a dream; yes, it was: "Be it so, if you will" (288). But what if such conclusions delusively evade yet reinforce the narrator's complicity with Satan, while easing readers away from the threat of demonic communion with themselves?

Just before the narrator retreats to the suggestion that evil is one man's dream, the Devil proposes that virtue is also a dream. " 'Depending upon one another's hearts, ye had still hoped, that virtue were not all a dream. Now are ye undeceived! Evil is the nature of mankind' " (287). "Virtue" can be historicized in the context of J. G. A. Pocock's *The Machiavellian Moment*, as republican civic virtue, or an ideology fostering elite male leadership. The ideology opposed, incorporated, and restrained commercial energies, often labeled "the passions and the interests," with a rhetoric mixing prudence, citizenship, resourcefulness, forcefulness, and manly honor, from the Florentine Renaissance through early American republicanism.[35] From Machiavelli onward, as Michael McKeon has emphasized, virtue was "a corrupted term," a question more than an answer, mediating tensions between ambitious new men and traditions of aristocratic honor. Eventually, detached from the patriarchal public sphere, it became relocated as a signifier of female chastity, the locus and refuge for elite male hopes of purified genealogy.[36]

Now, while a colonial Devil welcomes Puritans to the " 'mighty blood-spot' " (287) made by the passions and the interests, a colonial narrator welcomes his readers to a world extending the Devil's demystification of virtue. Both virtue and evil turn out to be dichotomous dream states generated by complex selves in hopes of "depending upon one another's hearts" to avoid scrutinizing their own. If progressive Protestant ministers have been teaching that evil and guilt are musty Puritan relics, the narrator will give his readers what they want to hear: Evil is also just a dream. The more insidious indeterminacy, however, is that evil is "if you will." In "Young Goodman Brown" and "Wakefield," each narrator recoils from the vision of heart-evil or social facelessness that he has contemptuously constructed. Yet the net effect leaves readers suspended in a willful, subjective indeterminacy.

4

In one way, the two stories comprising my final diptych, "The Celestial Railroad" (1843) and "Earth's Holocaust" (1844), reveal a road not taken in Hawthorne's romances: no women to speak of, naive and gullible narrators, hellfire and damnation climaxes, and explicit dependence on extrinsic texts – *Pilgrim's Progress* and the Bible – for moral authority. On the other hand, the stories show a clear shift toward satire in the uses of "Satan may take them." Mocking the philistine literary marketplace recurrently grounds the stories' broader indictment of social progress. Moreover, the first-person narrators not only parody the "liberal" and "enlightened" values of contemporary progressive readers, but also expose the demonic dangers latent in conventional sympathy. By implication, the romance narrations extend Hawthorne's serious play with his readers' enlightened liberalism.

"The Celestial Railroad" seems obviously derivative, since its allegory comes straight from Bunyan. Yet it transforms Christian's earnest moral struggle to a curiously whimsical satire, told by a nameless narrator who chooses the path of sociable ease and convenience. His ineffectual moral scruples reverse the balancing of social versus self-reliant alternatives in "Young Goodman Brown" and "Wakefield." When the narrator dares trust his own senses, his eyes, ears, nose, and heart palpitations tell him what his "liberal curiosity" (808) cannot, that demons are nearby, along with "my own sins that appalled me there" (816). When the pliable, accommodating cosmopolitan in him overrides the testimony of his

117

aching, bewildered brain, he becomes a representative observer of social complicities, from "the traveller of liberal mind and expansive stomach" (809) to himself nicely adjusting at Vanity Fair, the city that God has refused to incorporate.

There machines manufacture morality, capitalists consort with Lord Beelzebub, and the narrator has the "pleasure" of watching Beelzebub engage in "much ingenious skirmishing" with a miser for his soul, which the Devil at last obtains for sixpence, accounting himself the "loser by the transaction" (820). To borrow a label from Nathan O. Hatch's recent study of contemporary religious orators such as Lorenzo Dow, "communications entrepreneurs" are in full cry.[37] Eminent divines and lecturers now dispense such "omnigenous erudition" that all books have vanished. No one need "take the trouble of even learning to read" (818). True, persons oddly vanish from time to time, like the "soap-bubble" speculations of capitalism, but it all seems part of the general "trafficking for wealth and honors" (821). Though the narrator does feel uneasy about the "business," his curiosity about capitalist expediencies carries him into the new, improved "steam ferryboat" to Hell. The water's spray brings a traditional New England awakening of cold showers and virtue: "Thank Heaven, it was a Dream!" (824).

Not surprisingly, "The Celestial Railroad" proved instantly popular. It was avidly reprinted in various religious magazines throughout the 1840s.[38] Its popularity shows Hawthorne's growing skill in miming the contradictions of his readers, eager for self-improvement yet suspicious of self-reliance, and equally ambivalent about social improvements. Hawthorne has wittily reformed Bunyan's text to satirize reform. He has created his own ingenious narrative machinery, "liberally" updating Bunyan's names and devices. Displaying these devices as signs of Satan gone capitalist, he playfully capitalizes on his colonial source. Although a conservative satire of progressive liberalism seemingly stabilizes moral authority, the tale evokes an insouciant complicity with the spirit of enterprise, in tension with its ahistorical, antimarket moral. The irony of its marketplace success fits its contradictions.

"Earth's Holocaust," Hawthorne's Bonfire of the Vanities, fails where "The Celestial Railroad" succeeds, partly because it satirizes social reform with a more profoundly uneasy skittishness of tone about the literary marketplace. Yoking tall tale to apocalypse, it swerves to a grotesquely sentimentalized closure celebrating a holy text uncontaminated by readers' fingerprints. At first the world plays the role of the self-despising author in "The Devil in Manuscript." Taking Political Correctness to its logical extreme, it has resolved to burn every useless relic of the past, lighting an enormous bonfire set up on a Western prairie "at the representation of the Insurance Companies," for maximum audience without damage to property (887). That heavy-handed irony seems to stabilize the satire as a send-up of social progress.

The more interesting fault lines develop in the narrator, who has "a taste for sights of this kind," yet also seeks "some profundity of moral truth" (887). He turns out to be an author, anxiously aware of every bound volume fueling the unbound "volumes of smoke" (888, 901). He is also eager to trust the self-reliant moral authority of the "grave man" who "looked me in the face, by the kindling light" (887), when the narrator asks what has been used for kindling. Newsprint and magazines, the man finally replies, as if already aware of the narrator's preoccupation with print (887–8). Facing the narrator's self-interest, the grave man kindles questions about self-appraisal.

Unlike "The Devil in Manuscript," "Earth's Holocaust" frames hapless authors with the inexorable progress of history, explicitly from aristocracy to democracy, and implicitly from literature to oratory. All " 'the majestic distinctions of rank' " are thrown into the flames, despite a man "of stately presence," without intellectual power yet "born to the idea of his own social superiority," who pleads that traditions of rank and status brought civilization out of barbarism and nurtured " 'all the beautiful arts; – for we were their patrons' " (888–9). The sympathetic narrator has just signaled his own residual elitism with some snide remarks about the "plebeian spectators" who celebrate their "triumph . . . over creatures of the same clay and same spiritual infirmities, who had dared to assume the privileges due only to Heaven's better workmanship." On the other hand, "a rude figure" echoes the first paragraph of Emerson's "Nature," declaring that a man can at last advance by " 'force of character,' " not " 'by reckoning up the

119

mouldy bones of his ancestors!' " The narrator wavers, especially since the grave figure by his side seems pleased that such aristocratic " 'nonsense' " is gone, " 'if no worse nonsense come in its place.' "

Caught in the middle, the narrator continues to register a mixed response to the world's utopian contempt for the shackles of the past. He is clearly appalled by "the premature manliness of the present epoch," when a five-year-old boy throws his playthings into the fire (893). Yet he vigorously argues that " 'Reason and Philanthropy' " will make war obsolete, while a veteran soldier mutters about Cain and Abel (895). Earlier, as if endorsing the rhetoric of progress, the narrator notes that royal "rubbish" might have been suitable for the world's "infancy" and "nonage" but not for "universal manhood, at its full-grown stature," which "could no longer brook to be insulted." Evoking classic definitions of enlightened reason by Kant and Jefferson, these words also evoke the hot-headed excesses of fiery Tom Paine, especially when the crowd burns the regal costumes of actors as well (889–90).

Eventually the flames punningly change the meaning of "enlightened" (897, 903) into a demoniacal parody of the French Revolution. When "the world's entire mass of printed paper" is thrown into the flames, French texts "burnt red and blue, and threw an infernal light" on the spectators, "converting them all to the aspect of parti-colored fiends." The echo of "My Kinsman" also leads to a reassessment of Emerson, or at least of an Emersonian follower. As the narrator admires the "dazzling radiance" of Shakespeare's works in the flames, the critic beside him calls their loss a " 'benefit,' " since writers now will have to " 'light their lamps at the sun or stars' " (899).

Recoiling from the world's destruction of literature, the narrator grows increasingly antihistorical, though rather helplessly, as he discovers "my own works" have long since been vaporized (901). With a quiet intertextual bow to "The Devil in Manuscript," he beholds another "neglected" American author who "threw his pen and paper into the bonfire, and betook himself to some less discouraging occupation" (893). Yet the narrator takes care to mock the "desperate book-worm" whose " 'only reality was a bound volume' " (901). At last, in Hawthorne's most apocalyptic

"Satan may take them" finale, the narrator courageously takes sides – with the Bible.

" 'This is terrible!' – said I," as the people throw all the Bibles into the bonfire. These are "the main pillars, which supported the whole edifice of our moral and spiritual state." Amazingly, the pages "only assumed a more dazzling whiteness, as the finger-marks of human imperfection were purified away" (903–4). Absolute dichotomy restores transcendent meaning and authority, exposing history itself as the ultimate new-world vanity. A "dark-complexioned," red-eyed, demonic figure gloats about the heart's " 'foul cavern' "; " 'it will be the old world yet!' " (905). Once again the Devil and the human are nearly allied, through Adam's Calvinistic fall, untouched by every progress of the intellect.

The reactionary sentimentality here seems so fraudulent and evasive that most readers probably give the story up as a bad job, though at least one says the ending "expresses supremely" Hawthorne's Calvinist religious views.[39] Once again, however, contradictions undermine the seemingly pat conclusions. If Calvinism drives out enlightened liberalism, the Devil all but drives out God, whose text now has never been touched by human hands. It sounds more Manichean than Calvinist. While the pages "assumed" whiteness, the Devil's party assumes human hearts as well as bodies, by default. Moreover, the fantasy of God's purified textuality is just that: a hyperbolic transformation of an author's marginality into the cosmic authority of a Great Book without any readers. Finally, the vacuousness of the narrator's transcendent Bible-reliance not only bespeaks his flight from history's conflicts but empties out his dependence on external authority.

Earlier the moral weight given to the grave man's independence of mind masks contradictions explored in the narrator and polarized in the historical framing. Does the man represent old-style republican virtue, or new-style self-reliance? Residual aristocracy or incipient democracy? A hierarchy of social value and status, or universal manly character? Now the narrator is thrown back on his isolated subjectivity, with a kinder, gentler set of tensions. "How sad a truth – if truth it were –" he muses at the end (906). "Purify that inner sphere," or else any progress "will be a dream" as "real" yet "unsubstantial" as this bonfire, which perhaps has been "faithfully transcribed" and perhaps is only "a parable of my own brain!" Is the parable by, or about, his brain? The ambiguity throws him back on the same idle self that the Devil played with in "Young Goodman Brown."

5

Flagrantly missing from all these explorations of the tension between entrepreneurial self-reliance and colonial accommodations, whether to gentry values or canonical texts, is any complexity in women's voices. The first few paragraphs of "Young Goodman Brown" seem artfully poised between novelistic and allegorical uses of "Faith": Is she a young wife seductively afraid of herself, or a theological signifier? Thereafter, the story takes the theological high/low ground until its final psychological swerve, when the first paragraphs cast a residual shadow of doubt on the suggestion that it was all a dream. How could heart-evil be reduced to one man's problem, when his wife has voiced similar fears? Her voice complicates his indeterminacy, an echo without a difference. Mrs. Wakefield has moments of greater poignancy, or at least more depth than the narrator imagines for her husband's sluggish vanity. Like Mrs. Brown, however, she becomes a regretful interpretive adjunct to her man's adventure in autonomy.

By 1851, when Hawthorne was defining his genre not as allegorical tales but as "psychological romance," he was risking what T. Walter Herbert has called a "shamanistic" exploration of New England's gender codes.[40] In the romances, narrating women's rebellious passion licenses the full daring of the Satan-susceptible self as a trope for Hawthorne's ambivalence about both inwardness and creativity, especially with Hester Prynne and Zenobia. Paradoxically, he discovers that genuine self-reliance may be female, "the devil in the shape of a woman." Male self-absorption masks a will to power, which in turn masks a patriarchal self-colonization, whereas a woman's witchlike passions may be a site of rebellion from patriarchal values. By 1855, atoning for his insult to "scribbling women," Hawthorne praises the creative witchery of Fanny Fern, who "writes as if the devil were in her."[41] When it offers closure, the trope now seems primarily self-reflexive, as when

Jaffrey Pyncheon disintegrates into darkness visible, or when Hester terrifies herself with proud Francesca dreams of being married to Dimmesdale in Hell, or less containably when Zenobia dies with clenched hands, ready to rise "at the day of judgment" in the same posture of defiance.[42] For Hawthorne, self-reliance has come to license his own transgression of gender boundaries.

With a few notable exceptions, especially "Rappaccini's Daughter," such complexities of passion in male and female subjectivities do not threaten the more dichotomized tensions in the tales between moralizing narrations and brooding self-reliance. Instead, women either redeem men from themselves or function as victims and mirrors of men's narcissistic dominance. Hawthorne took a long time to realize that self-reliance was an opening to middle-class gender struggles, not just an ending to Eurocentric authority. Then psychological romance displaces colonial allegory. Like the romances, which often ventriloquize his readers' moral values, the tales affirm yet undermine precapitalist hierarchies of shame and virtue. As Richard Brodhead puts it, readers are left with "the Hawthorne that every literary institutionalization tends to contain: Hawthorne the doubt bearer, dissolver of the ground on which value of any sort could be determined."[43]

At the end of *The Inferno*, Dante tauntingly shames the Devil himself. After climbing down his huge body to the hip, the disoriented pilgrim looks back to see Lucifer's enormous legs sticking up in the air, as if the Devil were hanging upside down in one of the "defaming pictures" used by Dante's contemporaries to strip a man of honor and reputation.[44] Hawthorne uses Satan to invert self-reliance, defaming it as a mode of demonic possession. At the same time, he throws readers back on their subjective interpretations of Satanic or narrative authority to impose closure on their own subjectivity – what he called, in "Alice Doane's Appeal" (208), "the ceaseless flux of mind[.]"

"Satan may take them" therefore mediates among a good many historicizable tensions in Hawthorne's tales, as New England grew from postcolonial periphery to capitalist core of production. But it also establishes a place for ambiguity in a culture already eager to package meanings and subjectivities into easily marketable images. In the Persian language, ambiguity is called "two-heartedness."

According to Roy Mottahedeh's *The Mantle of the Prophet*, the Zoroastrian religion may have supplied Satan to the Old Testament, where darkness and evil slowly become represented as an active force, not just as the absence of light. A "belief in the many-faced subtlety of evil" has helped to create "the great interior spaces in which the Iranian soul has breathed and survived."[45]

In a culture still hell-bent on marketing, progress, and positive thinking, perhaps the most complex irony in Hawthorne's uses of the Satan-susceptible self is that thinking about evil gave his sensibility some breathing room. Whereas the Devil's delusiveness gave readers a way to evade the subjective nervousness aroused by Satan's accusations, it gave Hawthorne a way to enter his own interior spaces. From within, he could critique his culture, transgress himself, and affirm the play of meanings so basic to any life of the mind.

NOTES

1 Letter of March 13, 1821, to Elizabeth C. Hathorne, reprinted in *Nathaniel Hawthorne's Tales*, ed. James McIntosh (New York and London: W. W. Norton & Co., 1987), pp. 295–6. In *Dearest Beloved: The Hawthornes and the Making of the Middle-class Family* (Berkeley: University of California Press, 1993), chap. 5, T. Walter Herbert links this letter to another letter to Hawthorne's mother almost a year earlier (March 17, 1820): "Why was I not a girl that I might have been pinned all my life to my Mother's apron." Herbert emphasizes Hawthorne's wish to establish a "girlish" and aristocratic leisure space for himself, at odds with conventionally masculine pressures to choose a profession. In Hawthorne's youthful novel *Fanshawe*, however, a "dream of undying fame...more powerful than a thousand realities" lies in the "inmost heart" of the autobiographical hero. Nathaniel Hawthorne, *Novels*, ed. Millicent Bell (New York: The Library of America, 1983), p. 18.

2 In *New England Literary Culture: From Revolution through Renaissance* (Cambridge: Cambridge University Press, 1986), Lawrence Buell teases out some complex ironies in Hawthorne's representations of neoclassic didacticism (e.g., pp. 66–8, 100–2).

3 Nathaniel Hawthorne, *Tales and Sketches*, ed. Roy Harvey Pearce (New

York: The Library of America, 1982). This edition, like the Library of America *Novels,* replicates the text of the *Centenary Edition of the Works of Nathaniel Hawthorne,* eds. William Charvat, Roy Harvey Pearce, and Claude M. Simpson (Columbus: Ohio State University Press, 1962–). Further references to Hawthorne's tales and sketches will be cited from this text. I should note that a close comparison with the texts reproduced from early magazine printings in the Norton *Tales,* ed. McIntosh, shows numerous differences in punctuation from the Centenary text.

4 On Calvinism and social change, see David G. Hackett, *The Rude Hand of Innovation: Religion and Social Order in Albany, New York, 1652–1836* (New York and Oxford: Oxford University Press, 1991), esp. chap. 3, and Nathan O. Hatch, *The Democratization of American Christianity* (New Haven and London: Yale University Press, 1989), esp. pp. 40–3, 170–9, 196–7. In *Puritan Legacies: Paradise Lost and the New England Tradition, 1630–1890* (Ithaca and London: Cornell University Press, 1987), Keith W. F. Stavely concludes that Satan represents both modernism and capitalism, as Milton foresaw (p. 273, also pp. 71–97, 214–16).

On Hawthorne's fascination with fires, see James R. Mellow, *Nathaniel Hawthorne in His Times* (Boston: Houghton Mifflin Co., 1980), pp. 44–6. In *Rediscovering Hawthorne* (Princeton: Princeton University Press, 1977), Kenneth Dauber argues in passing that "all Hawthorne's devils" represent "the unconscious, projected outside" (75), with anal transformations of anger.

5 On the rhetoric of Christian nurturance and maternal domesticity, see Colleen McDonnell, *The Christian Home in Victorian America 1840–1900* (Bloomington: Indiana University Press, 1986); Ann Taves, "Mothers and Children and the Legacy of Mid-nineteenth Century American Christianity," *Journal of Religion,* 67 (1987), 203–19; and Ann Douglas, *The Feminization of American Culture* (New York: Alfred A. Knopf, 1977), among many other studies.

6 Francis Henry Underwood, "Nathaniel Hawthorne" (1887), reprinted in *Hawthorne Among His Contemporaries . . . ,* ed. Kenneth Walter Cameron (Hartford: Transcendental Books, 1968), pp. 300–4, quotation p. 300. See also p. 301: "There was a great change in the community beginning about the time he reached manhood – a change which was the precursor of the literary awakening, which I have elsewhere called 'The New England Renaissance.' " Barrett Wendell apparently áppropriated or reinvented the phrase, before Harry Levin suggested it anew to F. O Matthiessen; Nina Baym credits Wendell in "Early Histories

of American Literature: A Chapter in the Institution of New England,"
American Literary History, 1 (Fall 1989), 476.

7 Richard H. Brodhead, *The School of Hawthorne* (New York and Oxford:
Oxford University Press, 1986), pp. 34–5. Satan's modern biographer,
Jeffrey Burton Russell, breezily asserts that "American writers tended
to detach serious studies of evil from the Devil, relegating him to tales of
whimsy or horror stories." *The Prince of Darkness: Radical Evil and the
Power of Good in History* (Ithaca: Cornell University Press, 1988), p. 237.

8 On the tendency to disparage allegory, see Nina Baym, *Novels, Readers,
and Reviewers: Responses to Fiction in Antebellum America* (Ithaca and
London: Cornell University Press, 1984), pp. 91–3; also Edwin M.
Eigner, *The Metaphysical Novel in England and America: Dickens, Bulwer,
Hawthorne, Melville* (Berkeley: University of California Press, 1978),
esp. p. 71.

9 Gregory Vlastos, *Socrates, Ironist and Moral Philosopher* (Ithaca: Cornell
University Press, 1991), esp. chap. 1 on Socratic irony, e.g., p. 31:
Complex irony "both is and isn't what is meant . . . true in one sense,
false in another." It forces listeners/readers to accept the "burden of
interpretation" despite themselves, "the burden of freedom which is
inherent in all significant communication" (p. 44).

10 Among new historicist studies presuming a national rather than regional antebellum hegemony, Sacvan Bercovitch's influential "Hawthorne's A-Morality of Compromise," *Representations*, 24 (Fall 1988),
1–27, has been expanded into *The Office of The Scarlet Letter* (Baltimore:
Johns Hopkins University Press, 1991). A provocatively different study
arguing that Hawthorne explores alien, "tourist," and utopian alternatives to a patriarchal "national symbolic" enacting its stresses on
the male body is Lauren Berlant's *The Anatomy of National Fantasy:
Hawthorne, Utopia, and Everyday Life* (Chicago and London: University
of Chicago Press, 1991). Joel Pfister's fine complementary analysis,
*The Production of Personal Life: Class, Gender, and the Psychological in
Hawthorne's Fiction* (Stanford: Stanford University Press, 1991), argues
that "the psychological" as an interpretive category is produced by
the "hothouse" middle-class family (pp. 51, 183). Hawthorne replicates and critiques that dynamic. Since gender roles are "lived allegories" (p. 47), Hawthorne's tales use allegory to critique male
monomaniacs who force women to read themselves as "wax angels
with bloodless bodies" (p. 42).

11 Bercovitch, "A-morality," p. 9; *Office*, p. 89, nicely transposing Clif-
ford Geertz's emphasis on "thick description" in anthropological
fieldwork.

12 Michael McKeon, *The Origins of the English Novel, 1600–1740* (Baltimore: Johns Hopkins University Press, 1987), e.g., pp. 297, 173–4, also pp. 162–71 on tensions between status and class criteria. My reading of Hawthorne requires two cross-Atlantic modifications of McKeon's neo-Marxist frame. First, New England grew from market periphery to capitalist core. Second, the transformation produced a gendered by-product, a regional marketplace constituency for literature, middle-class readers, especially women, who valued "absorbing" and self-disciplining novels. See Richard H. Brodhead's Foucauldian essay, "Sparing the Rod: Discipline and Fiction in Antebellum America," *Representations*, 21 (Winter 1988), 67–96.

13 The Centenary edition has "a universal hum" (p. 228); McIntosh, *Tales,* following the *Token*'s first printing of "My Kinsman," has "an universal hum" (p. 16). I use the first version here because I like it better.

14 Ronald P. Formisano, *The Transformation of Political Culture: Massachusetts Parties, 1790s–1840s* (New York and Oxford: Oxford University Press, 1983), pp. 26–9, 65–7, 298–301.

15 O'Sullivan quoted in Edwin Haviland Miller, *Salem Is My Dwelling Place: A Life of Nathaniel Hawthorne* (Iowa City: University of Iowa Press, 1991), pp. 149–50. On Democrats as "Periphery," Formisano, *Transformation,* p. 20; also Daniel Walker Howe, *The Political Culture of the American Whigs* (Chicago and London: University of Chicago Press, 1979), esp. p. 32 and chap. 5, on Whigs and "The Entrepreneurial Ethos" (pp. 96–122). Lawrence Frederick Kohl, in *The Politics of Individualism: Parties and the American Character in the Jacksonian Era* (New York and Oxford: Oxford University Press, 1989), argues that both the Democrats and the Whigs constitute "outsider" and "insider" responses to individualism (pp. 228–9; also pp. 147–8, 63, 69–78 on Whig self-control; 35, 68, 21–2 on Democrats as outsiders).

16 Underwood, "Hawthorne," p. 302. Gloria C. Erlich emphasizes Hawthorne's reliance on practical, manly friends; she links such friendships to Hawthorne's ambivalence about Robert Manning, his dominant uncle. See *Family Themes and Hawthorne's Fiction: The Tenacious Web* (New Brunswick: Rutgers University Press, 1984), pp. 124–6, also pp. xvii, 59–60, 68–73, 117–19.

17 *The Vision; or Hell, Purgatory, and Paradise of Dante Alighieri,* trans. the Rev. Henry Francis Cary, in *The Works of the British Poets,* vol. 45, ed. Robert Walsh, Jr. (Philadelphia: Samuel F. Bradford, 1822), p. 194. This translation repeats Cary's earlier English editions of 1814 and, following Coleridge's praise, 1819. The 1819 edition (p. 187) provides

a note to "sound obscene," inviting readers to compare the original with a passage in Aristophanes (given in Greek), but this invitation is withdrawn for his American readers. Henry Boyd's 1802 translation, which completely bowdlerizes the passage, is apparently the first full translation of Dante into English. For centuries, at least in anti-Catholic England, even Dante was not canonical.

Angelina La Piana, *Dante's American Pilgrimage: A Historical Survey of Dante Studies in the United States 1800–1944* (New Haven: Yale University Press, 1948), notes that Cary's translation was "the turning-point of Dante's fortunes in England" and America (p. 24). Edwin Haviland Miller's recent biography notes that " 'the voice of voices' " (Sophia's phrase for her husband) read Cary aloud to Sophia (*Salem,* p. 224).

18 His allusions make clear that, by the mid-1840s at least, Hawthorne knew the *Commedia* in detail. See J. Chesley Matthews, "Hawthorne's Knowledge of Dante," *University of Texas Studies in English,* 20 (1940), 157–65. It is much less clear when or whether he knew the Italian version. Julian Hawthorne notes that Hawthorne did know Italian by 1857. The Bowdoin library apparently did not have a copy of Dante while Hawthorne was there, nor did Hawthorne ever check out a copy of Dante from the local library (see Marion Louise Kesselring, *Hawthorne's Reading 1828–1850*. . . [New York: New York Public Library, 1949]), despite checking out Guicciardini and Machiavelli in the late 1820s. Presumably, therefore, he already had access to Cary's translation.

19 On the inscrutable gentleman, see Agnes McNeill Donahue, *Hawthorne: Calvin's Ironic Stepchild* (Kent, O.: Kent State University Press, 1985), pp. 205–9, arguing that he is "the most evil" of all Robin's antagonists, ushering Robin into the last circle of hell. Most critics portray him much more benignly.

20 As Michael J. Colacurcio points out in *The Province of Piety: Moral History in Hawthorne's Early Tales* (Cambridge, Mass., and London: Harvard University Press, 1984), demonic readings tend to oppose historical readings because the " 'High-Tory' " implications don't square with Hawthorne's later politics (p. 566, note; the critic is Alexander W. Allison). Cf. my own book, *Manhood and the American Renaissance* (Ithaca and London: Cornell University Press, 1989), pp. 231–9, for a more extended demonic reading; also Donahue, *Calvin's Ironic Stepchild.* In *Hawthorne's Divided Loyalties: England and America in His Works* (Rutherford: Fairleigh Dickinson University Press, 1987), Frederick Newberry argues that Hawthorne seeks a "recovery

of English traditions" throughout his career. His reading of "Kinsman" emphasizes Robin's father as a non-Puritan, ecumenical alternative to the anti-English mob (pp. 62–5).

21 *Compositions by John Flaxman . . .*, quotations trans. Rev. H. Boyd (London: Longman, Hurst, Rees, and Orme, 1807), p. 24: "The Lake of Pitch."

22 There have been many historicist readings of the tale, e.g., by James Duban, Peter Shaw, John McWilliams, and Bertram Wyatt-Brown. See Colacurcio, *Province,* pp. 130–53.

23 Letter of April 13, 1854, to James T. Fields, reprinted in McIntosh, *Tales,* p. 308.

24 Pages 389–92 of the Centenary edition, vol. 11, and p. 431 discuss the last-minute inclusion of "My Kinsman" into *The Snow-Image.* Brodhead's *School of Hawthorne* cogently illuminates Fields's role in staging Hawthorne's rise to canonical status in the early 1850s, inventing an "oeuvre" with which Hawthorne himself had to contend (pp. 54–7, 70).

25 Centenary edition, vol. 11, pp. 393–4. Duyckinck said the story should have had a supernatural ending instead.

26 Nina Baym, *The Shape of Hawthorne's Career* (Ithaca and London: Cornell University Press, 1976), p. 181. Q. D. ("Queenie") Leavis's essay is reprinted in McIntosh, *Tales,* pp. 358–71; it was originally published as "Hawthorne as Poet," *Sewanee Review,* 59 (Spring 1951), 179–205.

27 Poe, 1842 review of *Twice-Told Tales,* quoted in *The Recognition of Nathaniel Hawthorne: Selected Criticism Since 1828,* ed. B. Bernard Cohen (Ann Arbor: University of Michigan Press, 1969), p. 13.

28 Lawrence, *Studies in Classic American Literature* (Garden City, N.Y.: Doubleday & Co., 1951, first published 1923), p. 13; Baym, *Hawthorne's Career,* pp. 63–4, also pp. 53–4, 83, 142. In *Rediscovering Hawthorne,* Dauber links Hawthorne's allegorizing to elite community (pp. 14–15).

29 Cf. Hawthorne's preface to *The Snow-Image* (1851), which also contrasts the dangerous "inquest" or "burrowing" into a man's "essential traits" with the public's curiosity about an author's "external habits": "These things hide the man, instead of displaying him" (1154–5).

30 McKeon, *Origins,* p. 312. See also pp. 162–9, on the destabilization of status categories by "individualistic and class criteria" characteristic of "capitalistic or 'middle class' values" (p. 167); also pp. 295–314 on Bunyan.

31 Mellow, *Nathaniel Hawthorne,* p. 45, discusses "Oberon" and the

burning of Hawthorne's early manuscripts, though Miller, *Salem is My Dwelling Place,* suggests Hawthorne may have "overstated" (p. 93). It could be that he just burned his drafts.

32 Dashiell Hammett, *The Maltese Falcon* (London and Sydney: Pan Books, 1975, first published 1930), pp. 57–60. For Brodhead's phrase, see *Hawthorne, Melville, and the Novel* (Chicago and London: University of Chicago Press, 1976), p. 13.

33 Mark Twain, *The Adventures of Huckleberry Finn,* chap. 17 (the Grangerford house), ed. Walter Blair and Victor Fischer (Berkeley: University of California Press, 1985, first published 1884 [England], 1885 [U.S.]), p. 137. Most texts have a comma after "family."

34 For various readings of "Young Goodman Brown," see Colacurcio, *Province,* pp. 283–313, and Michael Davitt Bell, *Hawthorne and the Historical Romance of New England* (Princeton: Princeton University Press, 1971), pp. 76–81, both antiallegorical historicizings; David Levin's classic essay on specter evidence, "Shadows of Doubt: Specter Evidence in Hawthorne's 'Young Goodman Brown,' " *American Literature,* 34 (1962), 344–52; and Emily Miller Budick, *Fiction and Historical Consciousness: The American Romance Tradition* (New Haven: Yale University Press, 1989), pp. xi–xii, 85–97, which differentiates between dualistic male skepticism and relational female skepticism, analyzing "Young Goodman Brown" as an ironic exposure of the "moral absolutism and egocentrism" inherent in Brown's allegorizing (pp. 92, 90). If the self becomes a specter, the Devil becomes a seductive historian who makes the world confirm each man's delusive sense of specialness (p. 97). J. Hillis Miller takes this male-loner tradition to a skeptical extreme in his lengthy essay on prosopopoeia in "The Minister's Black Veil," *Hawthorne & History: Defacing It* (Cambridge, Mass.: Basil Blackwell, 1991). For Miller, the otherness of history becomes only the ahistorical threat of personal death; history is "an endless series of disruptive happenings," each personifying the absent/inanimate/dead to give the reader-I an illusion of sovereign life (pp. 124–5).

35 J. G. A. Pocock, *The Machiavellian Moment: Florentine Political Thought and the Atlantic Republican Tradition* (Princeton: Princeton University Press, 1975), reoriented a generation of historians and critics toward the history of republican civic ideas and ideology. Pocock does not do much with the emphasis on manly force and resourcefulness so flagrant in Italian Renaissance versions of "virtù," and latent in Enlightenment ideals of honor.

36 McKeon, *Origins of the English Novel,* esp. pp. 396, 185, 366–8, 384–5.

37 Hatch, *Democratization of American Christianity,* pp. 144–5 and *passim.*
38 On reprintings of "Celestial Railroad," see Mark Y. Hanley, "The New Infidelity: Northern Protestant Clergymen and the Critique of Progress, 1840–1855," *Religion and American Culture,* 1 (1991), 203–26, esp. 219–20. A Baptist weekly, *Christian Secretary,* reprinted it twice, in 1843 and 1847. For this reference I am indebted to David Hackett.
39 Donahue, *Calvin's Ironic Stepchild,* p. 193.
40 Herbert, *Dearest Beloved, passim.* See also Pfister, *Production of Personal Life,* on gender and class dynamics (e.g., pp. 184–5). Hawthorne's phrase, "psychological romance," comes from his Preface to *The Snow-Image,* reprinted in McIntosh, *Tales,* p. 292.
41 Hawthorne's letter to William Ticknor (February 1855); the passage has often been reprinted, e.g., introduction to Fanny Fern, *Ruth Hall & Other Writings,* ed. Joyce W. Warren (New Brunswick, N.J.: Rutgers University Press, 1986), p. xxxv. Cf. Carol F. Karlsen, *The Devil in the Shape of a Woman: Witchcraft in Colonial New England* (New York: Vintage Books, 1987), which emphasizes the Devil's cultural role as a displaced expression of women's resentments and desires for autonomous power (pp. 244–9), when faced with a new ideology requiring men to be mobile economic individuals and women to be self-sacrificing (pp. 180–1). Pfister, *Production of Personal Life,* p. 75, notes an earlier, contrary impulse in Hawthorne, who praised Sophia for never having " 'prostituted' " herself by being a scribbling woman; they " 'walk abroad the streets, physically stark naked.' "

   A fine essay by Monika M. Elbert, "Hawthorne's 'Hollow' Men: Fabricating Masculinity in 'Feathertop,' " *ATQ,* 5 (September 1991), 169–82, situates Hawthorne's last story in the domestic contradictions wrought by capitalism. Elbert argues that Hawthorne's changing uses of demonism express his growing fascination with powerful women who subvert the gender categories crippling men (p. 179).
42 Herbert, *Dearest Beloved,* suggests that Jaffrey Pyncheon diffuses into "darkness visible." In *Manhood and the American Renaissance,* pp. 264, 268, I argue that Hester secretly dreams of being married spiritually to Dimmesdale in Hell.
43 Brodhead, *School of Hawthorne,* p. 102.
44 On defaming pictures, see Samuel Y. Edgerton, Jr., *Pictures and Punishment: Art and Criminal Prosecution during the Florentine Renaissance* (Ithaca and London: Cornell University Press, 1985). The northern Italian genre flourished between 1200 and 1400. When males from the upper classes fled after being accused of either treason or fraud, authorities would often commission artists to paint shaming portraits

in public places. The greatest shame was to be painted upside down
(pp. 75–98).

45 Roy Mottahedeh, *The Mantle of the Prophet: Religion and Politics in Iran*
(New York: Pantheon Books, 1985), pp. 63, 155, 144. By the early
1840s at least, Hawthorne had become interested in Zoroastrian ideas
of dualism and evil; see Millicent Bell, "Hawthorne's 'Fire Worship':
Interpretation and Source," *American Literature*, 24 (March 1952), 31–
9, esp. 36–8.

6

Through a Glass Darkly: "The Minister's Black Veil" as Parable

EDGAR A. DRYDEN

He will keep the sayings of the renowned men: and where subtil parables are, he will be there also.

He will seek out the secrets of grave sentences, and be conversant in dark parables.

—Ecclesiasticus 39:2–3

Son of man, put forth a riddle, and speak a parable unto the house of Israel.

—Ezekiel 17:2

With him [Moses] will I speak mouth to mouth, even apparently, and not in dark speeches; and the similitude of the Lord shall he behold: wherefore then were ye not afraid to speak against my servant Moses?

—Numbers 12:8

Therefore speak I to them in parables: because they seeing see not; and hearing they hear not, neither do they understand.

—Matthew 13:13

AS A SELF-DESIGNATED "romance-writer"[1] (149) Hawthorne was fascinated by the theoretical implications of the generic mark; the problem of generic designations, which is a central concern in his prefaces, appears even more explicitly in subtitled designations as in *The Scarlet Letter: A Romance* or "The Minister's Black Veil: A Parable," the generic denomination I intend to explore in this essay. What exactly does it mean to say that "The Minister's Black Veil" is a parable? What is the relation between the title and subtitle? To what extent can the subtitle be seen as an interpretive clue to the reader that will allow him or her to place the text within a contextual order by establishing a set of generic expectations? These preliminary questions are complicated by the fact that the subtitle marking the story as parable is itself marked by a footnote giving the reader Hawthorne's historical "source" for the account of Parson Hooper.[2]

> Another clergyman in New England, Mr. Joseph Moody, of York, Maine, who died about eighty years since, made himself remarkable by the same eccentricity that is here related of the Reverend Mr. Hooper. In his case, however, the symbol had a different import. In early life he had accidentally killed a beloved friend; and from that day till the hour of his own death, he had hid his face from men. (371)

The curious relation between the story's subtitle and the footnote that purports to explain it offers a fitting entrance to the shadowy world of "The Minister's Black Veil." In parables as in fables we usually find " 'statements of fact, which do not even pretend to be historical, used as vehicles for the exhibition of a general truth.' "[3] And yet Hawthorne asks us to see Mr. Hooper as an historical figure or at least to view him as the literary copy of a historical original whose eccentricity is the source that will partially explain the eccentricity of the fictional character.[4] In the case of Mr. Moody the "import" of the symbolic veil is clear: It is the sign of the shame and guilt he feels at having "accidentally killed a beloved friend." In the case of Mr. Hooper, however, the reasons for his donning the veil remain "unaccountable" (372), and it becomes a "material emblem" (379–80) whose meaning remains to the end obscure. In both cases the crucial relationship is that between figural connotation and literal reference, a relationship that seems clear and uncomplicated in the case of the historical Mr. Moody but aberrant and threatening for the fictional Mr. Hooper, whose life is radically disturbed by the horrible irony that "only a material emblem had separated him from happiness" (379–80). One could say that the space that separates Reverend Hooper's "simple piece of crape" (373) from the "mystery which it obscurely typifies" (384) is analogous to that which distances the historical Mr. Moody from the fictional character who in some obscure way represents him. This ironic distance is marked in the story by the "faint, sad smile" that "glimmer[s] from [the] obscurity" (383) of the "double fold of crape" (378), a smile that is Hooper's only response to all questions as to his motives for putting it on. And those motives certainly seem obscure. The narrator, like Hooper, offers no specific explanation for the character's unaccountable behavior, although the generic mark inscribed by the story's subtitle suggests that Hooper's actions may have a scriptural or institutional precedent that may be more helpful than the factual one suggested by the footnote. And indeed the Bible seems to suggest several possibilities.[5]

When Moses returns to the children of Israel after spending forty days and forty nights in the presence of God "the skin of his face shone; and they were afraid to come nigh him" (Exodus 34:30) until Moses "put a vail on his face" (Exodus 34:33), a "vail" that he removes when he enters the tabernacle to speak with the Lord. This act of veiling, like that of the Reverend Mr. Hooper, becomes the object of an elaborate figural reading, as in Paul's letters to the Corinthians.

> But if the ministration of death, written *and* engraven in stones, was glorious, so that the children of Israel could not steadfastly behold the face of Moses for the glory of his countenance; which *glory* was to be done away:
>
> How shall not the ministration of the spirit be rather glorious?...
>
> For if that which is done away *was* glorious, much more that which remaineth *is* glorious.
>
> Seeing then that we have such hope, we use great plainness of speech:
>
> And not as Moses, *which* put a vail over his face, that the children of Israel could not steadfastly look to the end of that which is abolished:
>
> But their minds were blinded: for until this day remaineth the same vail untaken away in the reading of the old testament; which *vail* is done away in Christ.
>
> But even unto this day, when Moses is read, the vail is upon their heart.
>
> Nevertheless when it shall turn to the Lord, the vail shall be taken away.
>
> Now the Lord is that Spirit: and where the Spirit of the Lord *is*, there *is* liberty.
>
> But we all, with open face beholding as in a glass the glory of the Lord, are changed into the same image from glory to glory, *even* as by the Spirit of the Lord.
>
> II Corinthians 3:7–18

This passage concludes the complex figure of reading and writing that structures the third chapter of II Corinthians, a figure that turns on the distinction between the spirit and the letter: *"Forasmuch as ye are* manifestly declared to be the epistle of Christ ministered by us, written not with ink but with the spirit of the living God; and not in tables of stone, but in the fleshy tables of the heart" (3:3). According to a nineteenth-century commentary of the sort Hawthorne would have known, St. Paul was the

> ministering pen or other instrument of writing as well as the ministering bearer and presenter of the letter. "Not with ink" stands in contrast to the letters of commendation which "some" at Corinth (v. 1) used. *Ink* is also used here to include all outward materials for writing, such as the Sinaitic tables of stone were. These, however were not written with ink, but "graven" by the "finger of God" (Exodus 31.18; 32.16). Christ's epistle (his believing members converted by St. Paul) is better still: it is written not merely with the *finger,* but with the *"Spirit of the Living God,"* it is not the "ministration of death" as the law, but the *"living* Spirit" that "giveth life."[6]

Paul contrasts the clearness and fearlesness of the Apostolic teachings with the concealment and indirection of the Old Testament. And in doing so he

> passes from the literal fact to the truth symbolized by it, the blindness of Jews and Judaizers to the ultimate end of the law: stating that Moses *put on the veil that they might not look steadfastly at* (Romans 10.4) *the end of that* (law) *which* (like Moses' glory) *is done away.* Not that *Moses* had this *purpose;* but often God attributes to His prophets the purpose which he has himself. Because the Jews *would not see,* God judicially gave them up *so as not to see.* The glory of Moses' face is antitypically Christ's glory shining behind the veil of legal ordinances. The veil which has been taken off to the believer is left on to the unbelieving Jew, so that he should not see.... He stops short at the letter of the law, not seeing the end of it. The evangelical glory of the law, like the shining of Moses' face, cannot be borne by a carnal people, and therefore remains veiled to them until the spirit come to take away the veil. (Jamieson, vol. 2, p. 305)

And when that occurs "Christians, as contrasted with the Jews who have a *veil* on their hearts, answering to Moses' veil on his face," will stand with open face "changed into His image by beholding Him" (Jamieson, vol. 2, p. 305).

As this commentary suggests, figural reading such as Paul's is itself a form of veiling that requires in its turn careful interpretation. When he figures himself as an instrument of writing and the lives of his converts as epistles from Christ able to be read by all men, he is speaking parabolically, and the parables in both the Old and New Testaments are dark sayings where one thing is expressed in terms of something else so that it demands attention and insight, sometimes an actual explanation (Smith, vol. 3, p. 2328). Associated with the dark sayings of rabbinic teachings, parables are linked with those things "darkly announced under the ancient economy, and during that period darkly understood, but fully published under the Gospel" (Jamieson, vol. 2, p. 43). But Christ's decision to adopt the parabolic mode complicates this distinction by calling attention to the generic resemblance between the form of his teaching and that of the rabbis.

> The parable was made the intrument for teaching the young disciple to discern the treasures of wisdom of which the "accursed multitude" was ignorant. The teaching of our Lord at the commencement of his ministry was, in every way, the opposite of this. The Sermon on the Mount may be taken as the type of the "words of Grace" which he spake, "not as the scribes." Beatitudes, laws, promises were uttered distinctly, not indeed without similitudes, but with similitudes that explained themselves. So for some months he taught in synagogues and on the sea-shore of Galilee, as he had before taught in Jerusalem, and as yet without a parable. But then there comes a change. His direct teaching was met with scorn, unbelief, hardness, and He seems for a time to abandon it for that which took the form of parables. The question of the disciples (Matt. xiii. 10) implies that they were astonished. Their master was no longer proclaiming the Gospel of the kingdom as before. He was falling back into one at least of the forms of Rabbinic teaching. . . . He was speaking to the multitude in the parables and dark sayings which the Rabbis reserved for their chosen disciples. . . . He had chosen this form of teaching because the people were spiritually blind and deaf . . . and in order that they might remain so. . . . Men have set themselves against the truth, and therefore it is hid from their eyes, presented to them in forms in which it is not easy for them to recognize it. To the inner circle of the chosen it is given to know

the mysteries of the kingdom of God. To those who are without, all these things are done in parables. (Smith, vol. 3, pp. 2328–9)

Biblical parables, in short, are veils that serve the double purpose of revealing and concealing, making manifest through their figural drapery and mysteries of the kingdom to those capable of knowing and relishing them and providing some temporary fictitious entertainment to those insensible to spiritual things. In this sense, parabolic, figurative language like the "double VEIL" that shrouds the Holy of Holies in the tabernacle, is a "dread symbol of *separation between God and guilty men*" (Jamieson, vol. 2, p. 61). It withdraws the light from those who love darkness and protects the truth from scoffers, but through the process of interpretation offers the possibility of direct access to divine presence. Those "who ask the meaning of the parable, will not rest till the teacher has explained it, are led step by step to the laws of interpretation, so that they can understand all parables, and then pass into the higher region in which parables are no longer necessary, but all things are spoken plainly" (Smith, vol. 3, p. 2329).

This happy crossing between literal and figural, between seeing and being, between the Old and the New Testaments, that the biblical text enacts is short-circuited in Hawthorne's parable which dramatizes a collision between literal reference and illustrative significance. The story opens with a description of communal life in a "real" town (Milford, Connecticut) where there seems to be a perfect solidarity of signs and meanings.

> The sexton stood in the porch of Milford meeting-house, pulling lustily at the bell-rope. The old people of the village came stooping along the street. Children, with bright faces, tript merrily beside their parents, or mimicked a graver gait, in the conscious dignity of their Sunday clothes. Spruce bachelors looked sidelong at pretty maidens, and fancied that the Sabbath sunshine made them prettier than on week-days. When the throng had mostly streamed into the porch, the sexton began to toll the bell, keeping his eye on the Reverend Mr. Hooper's door. The first glimpse of the clergyman's figure was the signal for the bell to cease its summons. (371)

Here is a world characterized by its smooth, untroubled surface, the result of the easy familiarity of the happily conventional, a world whose contents may be assumed to be unambiguously *given*.

The behavior of the people is as natural and fitting as the sunshine that illuminates their faces; and the figure of their clergyman whose arrival they await seems equally to confirm the shared awareness of a given, common humanity. A "gentlemanly person . . . dressed with due clerical neatness," he is, with one exception, entirely unremarkable. But that "one thing remarkable in his appearance" is enough to disturb the untroubled surface of the community by making him "strange" (371) and "unaccountable" (372). He has put on a black veil that seems to consist of "two folds of crape, which entirely concealed his features, except the mouth and chin, but probably did not intercept his sight, farther than to give a darkened aspect to all living and inanimate things" (372). The most immediate and drastic effects of this "simple piece of crape" (373), however, have nothing to do with the way it changes the minister's view of the world. Rather they result from the fact that it defamiliarizes him for his parishioners: " 'I can't really feel as if good Mr. Hooper's face was behind that piece of crape,' said the sexton. 'I don't like it,' muttered an old woman, as she hobbled into the meeting-house. 'He has changed himself into something awful, only by hiding his face' " (372).

> "How strange," said a lady, "that a simple black veil, such as any woman might wear on her bonnet, should become such a terrible thing on Mr. Hooper's face!" "Something must surely be amiss with Mr. Hooper's intellects," observed her husband. . . . "But the strangest part of the affair is the effect of this vagary even on a sober-minded man like myself. The black veil, though it covers only our pastor's face, throws its influence over his whole person, and makes him ghostlike from head to foot." (374)

Apparently the "horrible black veil['s]" (376) awful "influence" (374) derives from the fact that, in covering the face, it radically disfigures or defaces, making the minister an object of both morbid, idle curiosity and peculiar dread.

> His converts always regarded him with a dread peculiar to themselves, affirming, though but figuratively, that, before he brought them to celestial light, they had been with him behind the black veil. . . . Dying sinners cried aloud for Mr. Hooper, and would not yield their breath till he appeared; though ever, as he stooped to whisper consolation, they shuddered at the veiled face so near their

own. Such were the terrors of the black veil, even when Death had
bared his visage! Strangers came long distances to attend service at
his church, with the mere idle curiosity of gazing at his figure,
because it was forbidden them to behold his face. (381)

The effect of the veil is to make Hooper visible as being veiled,
to substitute for a "face to face" (373) relationship one where the
other is perceived "through a glass, darkly" (I Corinthians 13:12)
or enigmatically, that is to say, figuratively. On the one hand the
story insists on the literalness of the veil, that it is simply a physical
object (one "cause" of Hooper's sad, ironic smile is the recognition
that "only a material emblem had separated him from happiness"
[379–80]) whereas on the other, as the above passage suggests, it
becomes a figure for trope itself. Once Hooper uses it to cover his
face the double piece of crape can never again be simply its innocent existential self, for as a covering it becomes part of a system
of preestablished relationships, a system of figures invoked by the
story's subtitle, which points us to a world where material objects
stand for something other than themselves. When his converts
assert "though but figuratively" that they have been behind the
black veil they point to the process of comparison and substitution,
the chain of figures, that controls a system of representation. Or
to put the point another way: In the act of veiling his own face
Hooper reminds us of the ways in which we give a face even to
mute and senseless "Death" by incorporating it into the metaphoric chain of veiling and unveiling that energizes the story.

Indeed one could say that the veiled Hooper (a disfigured figure)
is an uncanny appearance, in the real world, of a figure, and as
such he disturbs the normal assumptions that govern the relationship between the literal and figural. The initial effect of his veiled
figure is to confuse, destabilize, and obscure. There is a "rustling"
and "shuffling" among his congregation "greatly at variance with
that hushed repose which should attend the entrance of the minister," and the veil throws its "obscurity between him and the holy
page, as he read the Scriptures" (373). "A subtle power was
breathed into his words" (373), but it is a power that darkens
rather than enlightens. "The people trembled, though they but
darkly understood him, when he prayed that they, and himself,
and all of mortal race, might be ready, as he trusted this young

maiden had been, for the dreadful hour that should snatch the veil from their faces" (375). Hooper is speaking figuratively here and doing so within a well established scriptural tradition, but the literal veil that covers his face prevents a traditional, untroubled response to his words. And his parishioners' reaction is echoed by the reader's when Hooper on his death bed "snatched both his hands from beneath the bed-clothes, and pressed them strongly on the black veil" in response to Reverend Mr. Clark's plea: " 'Before the veil of eternity be lifted, let me cast aside this black veil from your face' " (383). In these two examples the relationship between the literal and figural veils, as well as that between the acts of "snatching," is not a symmetrical one, and the lack of symmetry obscures the meaning of both even as it encourages further figuration. Plain, unadorned, nonfigurative speech becomes impossible — "It was remarkable that, of all the busy-bodies and impertinent people in the parish, not one ventured to put the plain question to Mr. Hooper wherefore he did this thing" (377) — even between the Reverend Hooper and his "plighted wife" (378).

> "No," said she aloud, and smiling, "there is nothing terrible in this piece of crape, except that it hides a face which I am always glad to look upon. Come, good sir, let the sun shine from behind the cloud. First lay aside your black veil: then tell me why you put it on."
> Mr Hooper's smile glimmered faintly.
> "There is an hour to come," said he, "when all of us shall cast aside our veils. Take it not amiss, beloved friend, if I wear this piece of crape till then."
> "Your words are a mystery too," returned the young lady. "Take away the veil from them, at least."
> "Elizabeth, I will," said he, "as far as my vow may suffer me. Know, then, this veil is a type and a symbol, and I am bound to wear it ever." (378)

With her eyes "fixed . . . steadfastly upon the veil" and "unappalled by the awe with which [it] had impressed all beside herself," Elizabeth is determined to see only what is there: "a double fold of crape" (378). But not even her "direct simplicity" can break the spell of the veil, for she too immediately is caught up in the system of figures that it generates. And her figure of speech — "let the sun shine from behind the cloud" — entangles her language and perception in the knot of analogies that complicates the narrative logic of "The Minister's Black Veil": Veil is to face as cloud is to sun, as night is to day, as time is to eternity, as body is to spirit, as words are to truth, and, most disturbingly perhaps, as face is to self. Many of the complexities of these associations must be put aside to be gathered up later, but it is important to note at this point that the focus is now on the problem of words and their meanings. Hooper's words like his face are veiled in the sense that they are figurative or parabolic expressions, public utterances that are the exoteric expression of an esoteric message. When he is asked by Elizabeth to unveil them, he does so by asserting the figural nature of the "piece of crape" but refusing to specify its meaning. The result is that she too is now enveloped by the veil's "terrors" despite Hooper's assurance that it is only a "material emblem" (380).

> "Have patience with me, Elizabeth!" cried he, passionately. "Do not desert me, though this veil must be between us here on earth. Be mine, and hereafter there shall be no veil over my face, no darkness between our souls! It is but a mortal veil – it is not for eternity! Oh! you know not now how lonely I am, and how frightened to be alone behind my black veil. Do not leave me in my miserable obscurity for ever!"
> "Lift the veil but once, and look me in the face," said she.
> "Never! It cannot be!" replied Mr. Hooper.
> "Then farewell!" said Elizabeth. (379)

The impasse here is the result of a sort of erosion of the distinction between literal and figural modes on which significance depends. Both Elizabeth and Hooper insist on the literal or material aspects of the veil, but neither of them is able to focus exclusively on it as a physical object. It is as if the "piece of crape" is always already figurative and thwarts all attempts firmly to fix its referential status. This sense of figurative excess is strengthened if the textual context is enlarged to include Hawthorne's other writings, for the veil is a figure that assumes a major structuring role in his world. As I have argued elsewhere, the question of the nature of the writer's identity is a central one for Hawthorne.[7] For him the relation between a writer's personal identity and the form of its manifestation to the world is a part of the larger problem of the relation between a human being's inner and social beings. More than most writers he is fascinated by the ways in which a writer's work is at once a veil that he wears and a manifestation of his most intimate concerns. The metaphorics of veiling do not creep into his text unreflectively. A "cloudy veil stretches over the abyss of my nature,"[8] he writes to Sophia, and most of his characters figuratively veil themselves in one way or another albeit without inspiring the dread that the Reverend Hooper does. Holgrave, for example, "habitually masked whatever lay near his heart" by his "New England reserve" (610), and Zenobia's pseudonymity is "a sort of mask in which she comes before the world, retaining all the privileges of privacy – a contrivance . . . like the white drapery of the Veiled Lady, only a little more transparent" (637).

As author, Hawthorne is as fond of veils as are his characters. His fascination with pseudonyms is well known – he used at different times M. de l'Aubépine, Oberon, and Ashley Allen Royce – and he published many of his early sketches either anonymously or under the signature of Nathaniel Hawthorne, having inserted a "w" in his family name at college. Fiction for him is a way of "opening an intercourse with the world" (1152) only in the sense that it is an appeal to "sensibilities . . . such as are diffused among us all. So far as I am a man of really individual attributes, I veil my face" (1147). Not even the apparently autobiographical figure of the prefaces can be taken as an unveiled version of the author. The writer's "external habits, his abode, his casual associates" are veils that "hide the man, instead of displaying him" (1154–5), and his characters too are veils or disguises that he wears. Coverdale, for example, as the "most extensively autobiographical character in Hawthorne's fiction"[9] is at once a manifestation of Hawthorne and a distortion that alters that manifestation. Hence in "The Custom House" he writes that "we may prate of circumstances that lie around us, and even of ourself, but still keep the inmost Me behind its veil" (121). The "veil" in this case is precisely that of figure, for the author ("keeping up the metaphor of the political guillotine") first asks that the sketch be

> considered as the POSTHUMOUS PAPERS OF A DECAPITATED
> SURVEYOR . . . and if too autobiographical for a modest person to
> publish in his lifetime, will be readily excused in a gentleman who

writes from beyond the grave. Peace be with all the world! My blessings on my friends! My forgiveness to my enemies! For I am in the realm of quiet! (156)

But as he announces the freedom that his "figurative self" enjoys, he reminds us that the "real human being with his head safely on his shoulders . . . had opened a long-disused writing desk and was again a literary man" (155–6). To be a "literary man," however, is also to wear the veil of figure. The narrator of "The Custom House" cannot be present in his own person but must appear as the "representative" (127) of others who are absent: his ancestors, his "ancient predecessor, Mr. Surveyor Pue" (156), even an earlier version of himself, a "scribbler of bygone days" (157). Substituting for self-presence, according to the "law of literary propriety" is the figure of a "literary man," a "romance writer" (149), and this figurative self, the self given by the act of language, is the only one locatable in Hawthorne's text. That self is always a veiled self, for it is an "I" or a subject represented by its signs or markers.

Thus, when Hooper dons his black veil his literal action repeats a biblical and literary figure but in a way that disturbs its status as a convention. His insistence that the veil is simultaneously literal and figural (a "material emblem" [380]) generates the uncanny wavering of a double reading that contaminates and breaks down the symmetrical chiasmus between the material and the emblematic. This disturbing wavering is most apparent in the associations between the veil and death, for death, since it cannot be experienced sensuously or psychologically, has to be expressed figuratively. The "hour" of death is the "dreadful hour that should snatch the veil from [our] faces" (375), and when the "veil of eternity [is] lifted" (383), "Death [bares] his visage" (381) and holds us in his "arms" (383). To speak of death as apocalyptic in the etymological sense of revelation or unveiling is to speak biblically and to anticipate that moment when all things are spoken plainly without the veil of similitude, but to give death a face and body is to figure or refigure it and to imply a necessary dependency on figurative language that defaces at the same time that it gives a face.

While his auditors shrank from one another, in mutual affright, Father Hooper fell back upon his pillow, a veiled corpse, with a faint smile lingering on the lips. Still veiled, they laid him in his coffin, and a veiled corpse they bore him to the grave. The grass of many years has sprung up and withered on that grave, the burial-stone is moss-grown, and good Mr. Hooper's face is dust; but awful is still the thought that it mouldered beneath the Black Veil! (384)

This passage is about a literal corpse, not about a figure for death or a figural representation of death. But the corpse is a veiled corpse, and as such it disrupts our conception of the literal as opposed to the figural by disturbing the system of analogies that energizes the text. When the veiled corpse is inserted in the chain of figures – veil is to face as body is to soul, as face is to self, as letter is to spirit, as veil is to corpse – the corpse occupies the position that face, soul, self, and spirit do in the system of analogies and disturbs the symmetrical structure of that system. When the corpse takes the place of the living body, the veil becomes the veil of a veil, the covering of a covering; it introduces the possibility that the face, the self, the spirit, the soul are figures. What is terrifyingly awful is the thought that veil and face decay together, for that thought reveals the literal as effaced figure and suggests that language works to cover up such effacements. To be told that Mr. Hooper's face turns to dust beneath the veil is to be reminded of the fact that Hooper's ''pale-faced congregation was almost as fearful a sight to the minister, as his black veil to them'' (373). Their ''pale visages,'' it appears, remind him of the ''visage'' of ''Death'' (381), for he is forced ''to give up his customary walk, at sunset, to the burial ground,'' because ''there would always be faces behind the gravestones, peeping at his black veil. A fable went the rounds, that the stare of the dead people drove him thence'' (380). The human face here no less than the sunset is a figure for death, the figure that fills the blank about which nothing can be said literally.

The human countenance, then, like the parable cannot be taken at face value, and therefore our situation as readers of ''The Minister's Black Veil'' is allegorically expressed by the situation of the characters in the story.[10] We, like Father Hooper's congregation, are denied a ''face to face'' (39) relation with the author who remains concealed behind the veil of the text, and he, like Hooper, insists at one and the same time on the text's material and emblematic status. Like *The Scarlet Letter*, ''The Minister's Black Veil'' is, on the one hand, "putatively historical...based on a reconstructed literal past" and yet on the other, it presents its actualities as signs or emblems[11] that signify something other than themselves and hence require interpretive action from a reader. In this sense Hawthorne's texts, like Christ's parables, seem to consist of a manifest carnal sense for the uninitiated outsider and a latent spiritual one available to the insider who has the benefit of special eye-opening knowledge and who therefore understands that the story cannot be taken at face value.[12] This certainly is the way Melville reads Hawthorne.

> The truth seems to be, that like many other geniuses, this Man of Mosses takes a great delight in hoodwinking the world. . . . But with whatever motive, playful or profound, Nathaniel Hawthorne has chosen to entitle his pieces in the manner he has, it is certain, that some of them are directly calculated to deceive – egregiously deceive – the superficial skimmer of pages.

Still, as Melville's essay suggests, it is not easy to articulate what the "eagle-eyed reader" sees in the text that is as "deep as Dante" except to say that it is a "direct and unqualified manifestation" of Hawthorne's "blackness,"[13] a response not unlike that of Father Hooper's congregation to his black veil. In a curious way Hawthorne's text appears to turn insiders into outsiders, as Christ's parables seem to do in Mark's rather severe account of them. Kermode points out that Mark uses "mystery" as a synonym for "parable" and implies that the stories are dark riddles that not even the disciples, the most privileged interpreters, can answer (Kermode, 46). In this sense the parable as a genre seems remarkably similar to Romance as Hawthorne defines it in his prefaces. Romance for Hawthorne offers a mode of communication that maintains a tension between the hidden and the shown, thereby insuring that something will always remain in reserve, either as an unformulated thought shaded by language or in the form of a veiled figure whose meaning is not explicitly signified. Consider, for example, Hawthorne's description of Dimmesdale's confession in "The Revelation of the Scarlet Letter": "With a convulsive motion he tore away the ministerial band from before his breast. It was revealed! But it were irreverent to describe that revelation" (338). Like the "multitude" with its "strange, deep voice of awe and wonder, which could not as yet find utterance, save in the murmur" that follows Dimmesdale's "final word" (339), the narrator finds it difficult directly to say what he sees, perhaps because what he sees remains shaded by the veil of figure even in the "mid-day sunshine" (341). Dimmesdale himself suggests as much when, after insisting that Hester's scarlet letter "with all its mysterious horror . . . is but the shadow of what he bears on his own breast," goes on to say that "his own red stigma, is no more than the type of what has seared his inmost heart" (338). No wonder then that "there was more than one account of what had been witnessed on the scaffold."

> It is singular, nevertheless, that certain persons, who, were spectators of the whole scene, and professed never once to have removed their eyes from the Reverend Dimmesdale, denied that there was any mark whatever on his breast, more than on a new-born infant's. Neither, by their report, had his dying words acknowledged, nor even remotely implied, any, the slightest connection, on his part, with the guilt for which Hester Prynne had so long worn the scarlet letter. According to these highly respectable witnesses, the minister, conscious that he was dying, – conscious, also, that the reverence of the multitude placed him already among saints and angels, – had desired, by yielding up his breath in the arms of that fallen woman, to express to the world how utterly nugatory is the choicest of man's own righteousness. After exhausting life in his efforts for mankind's spiritual good, he had made the manner of his death a parable, in order to impress upon his admirers the mighty and mournful lesson, that, in the view of Infinite Purity, we are sinner all alike. It was to teach them, that the holiest among us has but attained so far above his fellows as to discern more clearly the Mercy which looks down, and repudiate more utterly the phantom of human merit, which would look aspiringly upward. (340–1)

This "version of Mr. Dimmesdale's story" (341) suggests how seeing for Hawthorne is always interpretation in the sense that what is seen inevitably is taken as a sign standing for something else as in the case of a hieroglyph or a parable. And the meanings or "morals" which these signs "press upon us" must be "put . . . into . . . sentence[s]" (341) that become in their turn perplexing. Hence the "curious investigator" (the reader) who "perplex[es] himself with the purport" of the "semblance of an engraved escutcheon" carved on the "simple slab of slate" (345) marking the graves of Hester and Dimmesdale merely echoes the reactions of the "men of rank and dignity" who witness Dimmesdale's confession and are "perplexed as to the purport of what they saw" (336). This aspect of the human situation appears most clearly in the face of death (in Dimmesdale's "dying words" and in Hooper's "veiled corpse") for since death is nothing, our anguished anticipation of it, our attempt to articulate our relation to it, is necessarily oblique and parabolic.

For Hawthorne, then, the generic mark is not so much the sign of an aesthetic and/or historical category as it is a sort of epitaphic inscription that becomes a figure for story as such, that "Faery Land" realm inhabited by ghostlike presences that have a "propriety of their own" (633). Ordinary words like Hooper's veiled face "are a mystery" (378) because they are defamiliarized, detached from their referential function, from a present moment and a living "I," and hence presuppose as well as record the fact of death – in the case of "The Minister's Black Veil" that of the historical original, "Mr. Joseph Moody of York, Maine, who died about eighty years since" (371), that of Parson Hooper, Moody's fictional representation, and, finally, that of the author. Romance and parable are names for "Posthumous papers," fictional products of one "who writes from beyond the grave" (156), speaking monuments whose words like those inscribed on Hester and Dimmesdale's tombstone serve only to "perplex" the reader who is always the last surviving consciousness.

NOTES

1 All references to Hawthorne's fiction will be to the following editions: Nathaniel Hawthorne, *Novels,* ed. Millicent Bell (New York: The Library of America, 1983); *Tales and Sketches,* ed. Roy Harvey Pearce (New York: The Library of America, 1982).

2 For a discussion of the Reverend Moody of York, Maine, and his relation to Hawthorne's story, see J. Hillis Miller, "Literature and History: The Example of Hawthorne's 'The Minister's Black Veil,' " *Bulletin of the American Academy of Arts and Sciences* 41 (Feb. 1988), 20–1, and especially Frederick Newberry, "The Biblical Veil: Sources

and Typology in Hawthorne's 'The Minister's Black Veil,' " *Texas Studies in Language and Literature* 31 (Summer 1989), 171–83.

3 William Smith, *Dictionary of the Bible*, ed. H. B. Hackett (New York: Hurd and Houghton, 1871), vol 1, p. 807. I am using Smith's and other nineteenth-century works of biblical scholarship with the assumption that they will reflect Hawthorne's understanding of parable. Hereafter cited in the text as Smith.

4 This tension between historical and figural meaning is reflected in recent commentary on Hawthorne's story, which is seen, on the one hand, as the representation of a particular historical moment in the evolution of New England Puritanism (Michael Colacurcio, *The Province of Piety: Moral History in Hawthorne's Early Tales* [Cambridge: Harvard University Press, 1984], pp. 314–85, and Newberry, cited above, 169–95) and, on the other, as an expression of a linguistic turn in humanistic studies that concedes that language can no longer be understood as simply a medium for the representation of a reality outside itself (Miller, cited above, 15–31, and J. Hillis Miller, ''The Profession of English: An Exchange,'' *ADE Bulletin* 88 [Winter 1987], 41–8). My own reading resembles Miller's rhetorical one (I am especially indebted to his discussion of the trope of prosopopoeia in Hawthorne's text) but differs from his in suggesting that the generic mark offers at least a partial solution to the story's hermeneutical difficulties.

5 For two useful but different treatments of the biblical context of Hawthorne's story see Judy McCarthy, '' 'The Minister's Black Veil': The Concealing Moses and the Holy of Holies,'' *Studies in Short Fiction* 24 (Spring 1987), 131–8, and Newberry, cited above. Newberry's account is an especially suggestive one, but his reading differs from mine in seeing the story as a criticism of Father Hooper because his veil ''divides mortals from one another and from God, and . . . finally amounts to a profound anachronism whose emphasis on the age of Old Adam essentially renounces the availability of redemption through Christ's only historical appearance'' (189).

6 Robert Jamieson, A. R. Fausset, and David Brown, *A Commentary, Critical and Explanatory on the Old and New Testaments*, 2 vols. (Philadelphia: S. S. Scranton & Co., 1872), vol. 2, p. 304. Hereafter cited in the text as Jamieson.

7 Edgar Dryden, *Nathaniel Hawthorne: The Poetics of Enchantment* (Ithaca and London: Cornell University Press, 1977).

8 Nathaniel Hawthorne, *The Letters 1813–1843, The Centenary Edition of the Works of Nathaniel Hawthorne*, eds. William Charvat, Roy Harvey

Pearce, and Claude Simpson (Columbus: Ohio State University Press), vol. 15, p. 612.

9 Arlin Turner, "Introduction," Nathaniel Hawthorne, *The Blithedale Romance* (New York: W. W. Norton, 1958), p. 23.

10 On this point see Miller, "Literature and History," 45–6.

11 Millicent Bell, "The Obliquity of Signs: *The Scarlet Letter*," *Massachusetts Review* (Spring 1982), 10.

12 I am indebted here to Frank Kermode's discussion of parable in *The Genesis of Secrecy* (Cambridge: Harvard University Press, 1979), p. 4. Hereafter cited in the text as Kermode.

13 Herman Melville, *The Piazza Tales and Other Prose Pieces 1839–1860*, eds. Harrison Hayford, Alma A. MacDougall, and G. Thomas Tanselle (Evanston: Northwestern University Press, 1987), vol. 9, pp. 250–1.

Notes on Contributors

Millicent Bell is Professor of English, Emerita, Boston University. She is the author of *Hawthorne's View of the Artist* (1962) and the editor of the Library of America *Complete Novels of Nathaniel Hawthorne* (1983). She is also the author of *Edith Wharton and Henry James* (1965), *Marquand: An American Life* (1979), *Meaning in Henry James* (1991), and of numerous articles on American literature.

Carol M. Bensick is Assistant Professor of English, University of California, Riverside. She is the author of *La Nouvelle Beatrice: Renaissance and Romance in "Rappaccini's Daughter"* (1985) and has published essays on Hawthorne, including one on *The Scarlet Letter* which is included in *New Essays on The Scarlet Letter* (1985).

Michael J. Colacurcio is Professor of English, University of California, Los Angeles. He is the author of *The Province of Piety: Moral History in Hawthorne's Early Tales* (1984) and articles on Hawthorne and others, a contributor to the *Columbia Literary History of the United States* (1988), and the editor of *New Essays on The Scarlet Letter* (1985).

Edgar A. Dryden is Professor of English at the University of Arizona and the editor of the *Arizona Quarterly*. He is the author of *Melville's Thematics of Form: The Great Art of Telling the Truth* (1968), *Nathaniel Hawthorne: The Poetics of Enchantment* (1977), and *The Form of American Romance* (1988), as well as articles on Hawthorne and others. He is currently at work on a new book to be called *Herman Melville and the Formation of a Literary Career*.

Rita Gollin is Professor of English at the State University of New York at Geneseo, and past president of the Nathaniel Hawthorne Society. She is the author of *Nathaniel Hawthorne and the Truth of Dreams* (1979) and *Nathaniel Hawthorne: An Iconography* (1983), as well as articles on Hawthorne and others; and she is coauthor of *Prophetic Pictures: Hawthorne's Knowledge and Uses of the Visual Arts* (1991).

David Leverenz is Professor of English at the University of Florida, Gainesville. He is the author of *The Language of Puritan Feeling: An Exploration in Literature, Psychology, and Social History* (1980), *Manhood and the American Renaissance* (1989), and articles on Hawthorne and other American writers. He is the editor (with George Levine) of *Mindful Pleasures: Essays on Thomas Pynchon* (1976).

Selected Bibliography

Criticism of Hawthorne's tales and discussion of his art as a writer of short fiction can be found in numerous books and articles dealing either with the writer's works as a whole or with certain particular works. A list of some outstanding modern studies relevant to the tales is offered here. The Introduction and all the essays in this volume use the Library of America volumes of Hawthorne's writing, *Tales and Sketches*, ed. Roy Harvey Pearce (1982) and *Complete Novels*, ed. Millicent Bell (1983) for the text of quotations.

Adkins, Nelson F., "The Early Projected Works of Nathaniel Hawthorne," *Papers of the Bibliographical Society of America* (1945), pp. 119–55.

Baym, Nina, *The Shape of Hawthorne's Career* (Ithaca: Cornell University Press, 1976).

Bell, Michael Davitt, *Hawthorne and the Historical Romance of New England* (Princeton: Princeton University Press, 1971).

Bell, Millicent, *Hawthorne's View of the Artist* (Albany: State University of New York Press, 1962).

Bensick, Carol Marie, *La Nouvelle Beatrice: Renaissance and Romance in "Rappaccini's Daughter"* (New Brunswick: Rutgers University Press, 1985).

Berlant, Lauren, *The Anatomy of National Fantasy* (Chicago, University of Chicago Press, 1991).

Brodhead, Richard H., *The School of Hawthorne* (New York, Oxford University Press, 1986).

Cagidemetrio, Alide, *Fictions of the Past: Hawthorne and Melville* (Amherst: University of Massachusetts Press, 1992).

Colacurcio, Michael J., *The Province of Piety: Moral History in Hawthorne's Early Tales* (Cambridge: Harvard University Press, 1984).

Crews, Frederick, *The Sins of the Fathers: Hawthorne's Psychological Themes* (New York: Oxford University Press, 1966).

Crowley, J. Donald, "The Artist as Mediator: The Rationale of Hawthorne's Large-Scale Revisions in His Collected Tales and Sketches," in *Hawthorne and Melville in the Berkshires,* ed. Howard P. Vincent (Kent: Kent State University Press, 1968), pp. 79–88.

Daly, Robert J., "History and Chivalric Myth in 'Roger Malvin's Burial,' " *Essex Institute Historical Collections* 109 (1973): 99–115.

Dauber Kenneth, *Rediscovering Hawthorne* (Princeton: Princeton University Press, 1977).

Doubleday, Neal Frank, *Hawthorne's Early Tales: A Critical Study* (Durham: Duke University Press, 1972).

Dryden, Edgar A., *Nathaniel Hawthorne: The Poetics of Enchantment* (Ithaca: Cornell University Press, 1977).

Erlich, Gloria, *Family Themes and Hawthorne's Fiction* (New Brunswick: Rutgers University Press, 1984).

Feidelson, Charles, *Symbolism in American Literature* (Chicago: University of Chicago Press, 1953).

Fetterley, Judith, *The Resisting Reader: A Feminist Approach to American Fiction* (Bloomington: Indiana University Press, 1978).

Fogle, Richard Harter, *Hawthorne's Fiction: The Light and the Dark* (Norman: University of Oklahoma Press, 1964).

Gollin, Rita K., *Nathaniel Hawthorne and the Truth of Dreams* (Baton Rouge: Louisiana State University Press, 1979).

Gross, Seymour, " 'My Kinsman, Major Molineux': History as Moral Adventure," *Nineteenth Century Fiction* 12 (1957): 97–109.

Hoffman, Daniel C., *Form and Fable in American Fiction* (New York: Oxford University Press, 1961).

James, Henry, *Hawthorne,* in *Literary Criticism: Essays on Literature; American and English Writers,* ed. Leon Edel and Mark Wilson (New York: Library of America, 1984).

Leavis, Q. D., "Hawthorne as Poet," *Sewanee Review* 59 (1951): 179–205.

Martin, Terrence, "The Method of Hawthorne's Tales," in *Hawthorne Centenary Essays,* ed. Roy Harvey Pearce (Columbus: Ohio State University Press, 1964).

McDonald, John J., " 'The Old Manse' and Its Mosses: The Inception and Development of Mosses from an Old Manse," *Texas Studies in Literature and Language* 16 (1974): 74–108.

McWilliams, John P., Jr., " 'Thoroughgoing Democrat' and 'Modern Tory': Hawthorne and the Puritan Revolution of 1776," *Studies in Romanticism* 15 (1976): 549–71.

"Fictions of Merry Mount," *American Quarterly* 29 (1977): 3–30.

Marks, Alfred H., "German Romantic Irony in Hawthorne's Tales," *Symposium* 7 (1953): 274–305.

Miller, J. Hillis, *Hawthorne and History: Defacing It* (Cambridge, Mass.: Basil Blackwell, 1991).

Newberry, Frederick, *Hawthorne's Divided Loyalties: England and America in His Works* (Rutherford: Fairleigh Dickinson University Press, 1989).

Newman, Lea Bertani Vozar, *A Reader's Guide to the Short Stories of Nathaniel Hawthorne* (Boston: G. K. Hall, 1979).

Pearce, Roy Harvey, "Hawthorne and the Sense of the Past, Or the Immortality of Major Molineux," *ELH* 21 (1954): 327–49.

Person, Leland S., Jr., *Aesthetic Headaches: Women and Masculine Poetics in Poe, Melville, and Hawthorne* (Athens: University of Georgia Press, 1988).

Pfister, Joel, *The Production of Personal Life: Class, Gender, and the Psychological in Hawthorne's Fiction* (Stanford: Stanford University Press, 1991).

Shaw, Peter, *American Patriots and the Rituals of Revolution* (Cambridge: Harvard University Press, 1981).

Simpson, Lewis P., "John Adams and Hawthorne: The Fiction of the Real American Revolution," *Studies in the Literary Imagination* 9 (1976): 1–18.

Stein, William Bysshe, *Hawthorne's Faust: A Study of the Devil Archetype* (Gainesville: University of Florida Press, 1953).

Stoehr, Taylor, *Hawthorne's Mad Scientists: Pseudoscience and Social Science* (Hamden, Conn.: Archon Books, 1978).

Swann, Charles, *Nathaniel Hawthorne: Tradition and Revolution* (Cambridge and New York: Cambridge University Press, 1991).

Waggoner, Hyatt H., *Hawthorne: A Critical Study* (Cambridge: Harvard University Press, 1955).

Warren, Robert Penn, "Hawthorne Revisited: Some Remarks on Hell-firedness," *Sewanee Review* 81 (1973): 75–111.